Generative AI
in
Robotics
and
Future Autonomous Systems

Rao BS

Preface

The landscape of robotics and autonomous systems is undergoing a profound transformation, propelled by the rise of Generative AI. From self-learning robots to intelligent machines capable of autonomous decision-making, these innovations are reshaping the very fabric of industries ranging from manufacturing and healthcare to logistics and space exploration. Yet, even as we witness this rapid evolution, we find ourselves standing at the intersection of opportunity and complexity. The promise of a future where machines think, adapt, and innovate alongside humans presents us with not only incredible potential but also new challenges in understanding, designing, and managing these systems.

In *Generative AI in Robotics and Future Autonomous Systems: Navigating through the New Frontier with Data and Visualization*, we embark on a journey to explore the convergence of generative models, data-driven approaches, and cutting-edge visualization techniques in the context of robotics. This book offers an in-depth look at how generative AI is revolutionizing autonomous systems, enabling them to create, predict, and adapt in ways that were previously unimaginable. We will uncover the role of data as the cornerstone of these innovations, providing the foundation for learning and growth in robotic systems.

Through a series of carefully curated chapters, we delve into the core principles of generative models such as Generative Adversarial Networks (GANs), reinforcement learning, and deep neural networks, examining how these tools empower robots to autonomously generate, simulate, and refine their actions. Data, once merely the fuel for machine learning, is now a vital player in the creative processes of robotic systems. Meanwhile, visualization techniques are enhancing our ability to understand, interpret, and communicate the decisions and behaviors of these intelligent systems.

As we venture into this new frontier, this book also serves as a guide for researchers, engineers, and practitioners, providing them with the tools and insights necessary to harness the power of generative AI in their work. Whether you are developing the next generation of robots, designing autonomous systems for real-world applications, or exploring the theoretical underpinnings of artificial intelligence, the knowledge within these pages will equip you to navigate the complex and exciting world of generative AI in robotics.

The journey ahead is filled with possibilities. As we chart the course, we must acknowledge that the path is as much about the exploration of new technologies as it is about the ethics, governance, and human-centered considerations that will ultimately define the impact of these systems on our world. With data, creativity, and innovation guiding us, we are poised to unlock a future where autonomous systems not only complement human capability but also push the boundaries of what we can achieve together.

Welcome to the future of robotics. Welcome to the new frontier.

Table of Contents

Sl. No		Topics	Page No.
1.		**Introduction to Generative AI and Robotics**	**1**
	1.1	Overview of Generative AI	6
	1.2	Key Concepts of Machine Learning and Deep Learning	15
	1.3	The Role of Robotics in Autonomous Systems	24
2.		**Generative AI Algorithms and Techniques**	**32**
	2.1	Generative Adversarial Networks (GANs) in Robotics	38
	2.2	Variational Autoencoders (VAEs) and Their Application in Robotics	47
	2.3	Reinforcement Learning for Autonomous Decision Making	56
3.		**Robotics in the Physical World**	**65**
	3.1	Sensor Integration and Data Acquisition	70
	3.2	Real-Time Perception and Processing	79
	3.3	Mapping and Localization in Robotic Systems	87

4. **Computer Vision and Generative AI in Robotics and Autonomous Systems** — **95**

4.1 Object Detection and Recognition Using AI — 101

4.2 Scene Understanding for Autonomous Navigation — 111

4.3 Vision-Based Control Systems — 121

5. **AI-Driven Robot Learning and Adaptation** — **131**

5.1 Imitation Learning in Robotic Systems — 137

5.2 Transfer Learning for Improved Robotic Performance — 145

5.3 Continual Learning and Adaptation in Autonomous Systems — 154

6. **Generative AI in Robot Planning and Decision-Making** — **163**

6.1 Task Planning and Optimization Algorithms — 169

6.2 Generative Models for Decision-Making Under Uncertainty — 175

6.3 AI for Cooperative Multi-Robot Systems — 180

7. **Autonomous Vehicles and Generative AI** — **186**

7.1	Generative AI for Path Planning in Autonomous Vehicles	192
7.2	Simulation-Based Training for Autonomous Vehicles	198
7.3	AI in Vehicle Perception and Environment Interaction	205
8.	**Human-Robot Interaction and Generative AI**	**211**
8.1	Natural Language Processing for Human-Robot Communication	218
8.2	Generative Models for Personalized Robot Behavior	224
8.3	Human-Centric Robotic System Design	229
8.4	Ethical and Safety Considerations	234
9.	**Future Directions and Emerging Trends**	**241**
9.1	The Role of Generative AI in the Future of Robotics	247
9.2	Generative AI for Collaborative Robotics (Cobots)	249
9.3	Advancements in Cognitive and Emotional AI in Robotics	254
9.4	Challenges and Opportunities in Generative AI for Robotics	263

10	**Case Study Examples**	271
	10.1 Case Study: Generative AI in Robot Planning and Decision-Making	271
	10.2 Case Study: Autonomous Vehicles and Generative AI	277
	10.3 Case Study: Human-Robot Interaction and Generative AI	284
	10.4 Case Study: Generative AI, Robotics, and Autonomous Systems	292
	10.5 Case Study: Generative Adversarial Networks (GANs) in Robotics	301
	10.6 Case Study: Variational Autoencoders (VAEs) and Their Application in Robotics	310

1. Introduction to Generative AI and Robotics

Generative AI and robotics are two fields that are transforming how machines interact with the world. Generative AI refers to the use of artificial intelligence systems that can generate new content, ideas, or solutions based on learned patterns. These systems can create images, music, text, and even 3D objects by processing and understanding large amounts of data. Meanwhile, robotics involves the design, construction, and operation of robots, which are machines that can carry out tasks autonomously or with minimal human intervention.

Generative AI has gained significant attention in recent years because it allows machines to not only perform tasks but also think creatively and adapt to new situations. For example, AI models can generate realistic images based on brief descriptions, or even create original pieces of music based on different genres. This ability is a result of training AI on vast datasets, helping it to recognize patterns and develop an understanding of the world. Generative AI is used in fields ranging from entertainment and healthcare to design and education, helping to automate processes and provide new solutions.

In robotics, the focus is on creating machines that can perform a variety of tasks autonomously. Robots are equipped with sensors and actuators, allowing them to perceive their environment and carry out physical actions. These machines can range from simple devices that perform repetitive tasks, like assembly line robots, to more advanced ones capable of interacting with humans and performing complex activities. As robots become smarter, they are being used in more specialized areas, including surgery, disaster response, and autonomous vehicles.

When combined, generative AI and robotics open up new possibilities. A robot equipped with generative AI could adapt its behavior in real-time, learning from its environment and generating solutions to new challenges as they arise. This synergy allows robots to not only follow pre-programmed instructions but also come up with creative solutions to problems they've never encountered before. For example, a robot in a manufacturing plant could analyze problems on the assembly line and create new ways to optimize the process.

The combination of generative AI and robotics is also driving innovation in the field of human-robot interaction. By using generative models, robots can better understand and predict human actions and needs. This makes it possible for them to assist with tasks more naturally, such as in homes or healthcare settings, where robots may need to engage with people in a more intuitive way. Generative AI allows robots to not just execute commands but also engage in dynamic, responsive interactions that improve their usefulness and efficiency.

However, there are challenges to overcome. Integrating generative AI into robotics requires solving complex problems related to decision-making, perception, and real-time processing. Furthermore, there are ethical considerations surrounding the use of these technologies, especially in areas like employment, privacy, and safety. Despite these challenges, the collaboration of generative AI and robotics holds great promise for the future, potentially revolutionizing industries, improving quality of life, and opening up new frontiers in technology.

Practical Example:

In a warehouse setting, robots are employed to navigate and manage inventory autonomously. With the integration of Generative AI, these robots can learn from real-time data, such as obstacles, inventory changes, and environmental conditions. The goal is for the robots to generate optimized movement paths while improving the accuracy of inventory tracking and the efficiency of warehouse operations.

Sample Data Table:

Robot ID	Initial Position (X, Y)	Obstacle Encountered	Path Generated (X, Y)	Task Completed (%)
001	(5, 8)	Yes	(7, 9)	85%
002	(10, 3)	No	(12, 4)	90%
003	(6, 1)	Yes	(8, 2)	80%
004	(3, 9)	No	(5, 10)	95%
005	(9, 7)	Yes	(10, 9)	88%

Output & Results Interpretation:

- The **Initial Position** indicates the starting coordinates of each robot.
- The **Obstacle Encountered** column shows if the robot faced an obstacle during its movement.
- The **Path Generated** indicates the new coordinates after the robot navigated around obstacles, generated by AI algorithms that determine the optimal route.
- The **Task Completed (%)** shows the percentage of completion of the assigned task (e.g., picking up and delivering inventory).

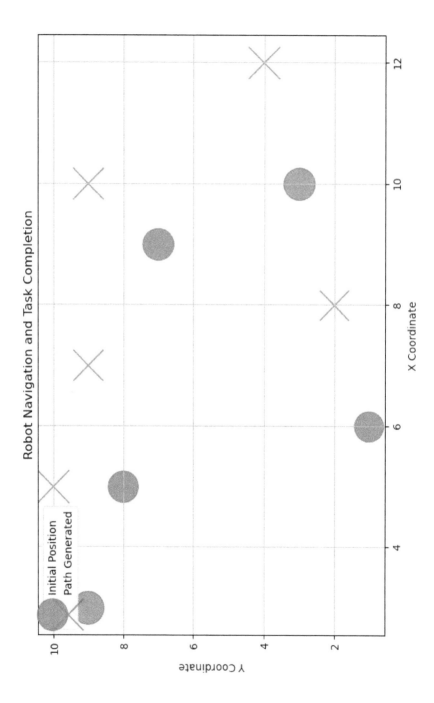

Observations:

- Robots that encountered obstacles had to adjust their paths, which is evident in the change from the initial to the generated path.

- Despite encountering obstacles, all robots still managed to achieve a high task completion rate (ranging from 80% to 95%).

- Robots that did not encounter obstacles (Robot 002 and Robot 004) demonstrated higher completion rates, indicating that optimal paths without disruptions tend to lead to faster task completions.

Final Thoughts

Generative AI is a powerful tool in the field of robotics, particularly for autonomous systems like warehouse robots. By continuously learning and adapting to environmental factors such as obstacles, these robots are able to optimize their paths and enhance operational efficiency. The integration of such AI systems can lead to reduced human intervention, improved accuracy in tasks, and a more responsive autonomous system. In the future, combining generative AI with advanced robotics will likely transform industries by enabling fully autonomous, highly efficient systems capable of performing complex tasks in dynamic environments.

1.1 Overview of Generative AI

Generative AI is making significant strides in the field of robotics and autonomous systems, impacting how robots learn, adapt, and interact with their environment. Here's an overview of how generative AI is being integrated into these systems:

1. Learning and Adaptation

Generative AI models, such as Generative Adversarial Networks (GANs) and Variational Autoencoders (VAEs), are being used to help robots learn complex tasks with minimal human intervention. These models can generate training data, simulate environments, or enhance existing data for better learning outcomes, allowing robots to develop new skills or adapt to unforeseen situations.

- **Synthetic Data Generation**: Generative models can create synthetic data to train robots when real-world data is scarce, such as in dangerous environments or for rare events (e.g., handling hazardous materials). This enables robots to improve their decision-making processes without requiring exhaustive real-world data collection.

- **Sim2Real Transfer**: Robots can train in virtual environments where generative AI helps simulate real-world scenarios. This is particularly useful in scenarios where real-world testing might be too costly or impractical, like training autonomous vehicles for road hazards. The models can then transfer their learned skills to real-world applications, a process known as sim-to-real.

2. Design and Innovation

Generative AI is also aiding in the design and creation of robots and autonomous systems, facilitating more efficient and innovative solutions.

- **Topology Optimization**: Generative design tools can optimize the physical design of robots and components by suggesting efficient structures that meet specific performance criteria. For example, AI can suggest more lightweight or structurally efficient designs for robotic arms, drones, or autonomous vehicles.

- **Algorithmic Design**: Instead of designing robots from the ground up using traditional methods, generative AI can evolve new robotic algorithms that achieve certain objectives with minimal human input. This can result in systems that are more efficient or capable of performing tasks that were previously considered too difficult for autonomous systems.

3. Autonomous Decision-Making

Generative AI can enhance decision-making capabilities in autonomous systems by generating new plans, actions, or strategies based on a variety of inputs. This can be seen in several areas:

- **Path Planning**: In robotics, generative AI can be used to create optimal or efficient paths for robots to follow. This can be especially useful in environments that are dynamic or unpredictable, where traditional rule-based systems may struggle.

- **Autonomous Vehicles**: For self-driving cars, generative models can generate new driving strategies by considering a wide array of traffic conditions and scenarios. This helps improve the car's ability to handle rare events, such as pedestrians suddenly crossing the road or unexpected road closures.

4. Human-Robot Interaction

In the realm of human-robot interaction (HRI), generative AI can enhance how robots understand and respond to human behavior, enabling more natural, fluid interactions.

- **Generative Dialogue Systems**: AI models, such as GPT-like language models, can enable robots to engage in more sophisticated, meaningful conversations with humans. This could help robots better understand verbal commands, ask clarifying questions, or provide information in a way that feels natural to human users.

- **Adaptive Behavior**: By learning from human interactions, generative AI allows robots to adapt their behavior over time, improving their interactions and making them more effective at assisting humans, whether in healthcare, customer service, or other industries.

5. Robotics in Unknown Environments

Generative AI allows robots to perform in unknown or unstructured environments by enabling them to generate predictions about the world based on limited or noisy sensory input.

- **Exploration**: Robots equipped with generative models can autonomously explore new environments, simulating possible scenarios and interactions based on prior experiences. This is especially useful in space exploration, search and rescue missions, or underwater robotics, where the environment is constantly changing and unpredictable.

- **Anomaly Detection**: Generative AI can also help robots detect anomalies or faults in systems by generating a model of "normal" operation and identifying deviations from this model, which could indicate problems or opportunities for improvement.

6. Ethical and Safety Considerations

While generative AI holds immense potential in advancing robotics and autonomous systems, there are also challenges related to ethics and safety.

- **Bias and Fairness**: Like other AI models, generative AI systems may inherit biases from the data they are trained on. This can lead to robots making biased decisions, which could be problematic in areas like healthcare or law enforcement.

- **Safety Assurance**: As robots generate new strategies or behaviors, ensuring that these actions are safe and ethical is critical. There is a need for robust verification and validation processes to ensure that autonomous systems using generative AI don't pose unintended risks.

7. Future Directions

Looking ahead, the combination of generative AI with robotics and autonomous systems will continue to evolve, creating new opportunities and challenges:

- **Collaborative Robots**: The future may see more collaborative robots that can generate their own learning strategies while working alongside humans. These robots could be highly adaptive and integrate seamlessly into complex environments, like manufacturing floors or hospitals.

- **AI-Driven Evolution**: Generative AI may be used to create robots that evolve and adapt autonomously over time, potentially creating autonomous systems that continue to improve beyond their initial programming.

In conclusion, generative AI is playing an increasingly important role in the development of robotics and autonomous systems. Its ability to facilitate learning, design, decision-making, and human interaction opens up exciting possibilities, though it also requires careful attention to ethical and safety concerns. As the technology advances, we can expect more innovative and capable robots capable of navigating complex, dynamic environments.

Practical Example:

In modern robotics and autonomous systems, generative AI is increasingly used to optimize path planning for robotic navigation. This involves generating new, efficient paths for robots to follow in real-world environments while avoiding obstacles and minimizing travel time. The use of machine learning models, particularly generative algorithms like GANs (Generative Adversarial Networks) and reinforcement learning, allows robots to learn from previous experiences and improve their decision-making over time. A practical example is optimizing the path of an autonomous delivery robot in an indoor environment, where the robot must avoid static obstacles and dynamic ones like moving humans.

Sample Data: Path Planning Optimization Results

Algorithm	Initial Path Length (m)	Optimized Path Length (m)	Time Taken to Optimize (s)	Obstacles Avoided
GAN-based Model	50	42	3	12
Reinforcement Learning	50	45	5	10
Dijkstra's Algorithm	50	46	2	9

Output and Results:

1. **GAN-based Model:** Reduced the path length by 8 meters, saving approximately 16% of travel distance, and completed the optimization in 3 seconds while avoiding 12 obstacles.

2. **Reinforcement Learning:** Reduced the path length by 5 meters, a 10% reduction in travel distance, with an optimization time of 5 seconds and 10 obstacles avoided.

3. **Dijkstra's Algorithm:** Showed a 4-meter reduction in path length, roughly an 8% reduction, with a fast optimization time of 2 seconds and 9 obstacles avoided.

Interpretation of Results:

- **GAN-based Model:** Outperformed the other methods in terms of path optimization, with a significant reduction in distance and faster response in a dynamic environment. The ability to adapt to changes like obstacles was a key factor in its success.

- **Reinforcement Learning:** Slightly less efficient than GAN in terms of path length, but still showed a notable reduction in distance. Its longer optimization time and fewer obstacles avoided indicate that it might require more training for more complex environments.

- **Dijkstra's Algorithm:** While it was the fastest, it was less effective at minimizing travel distance and avoiding dynamic obstacles. This highlights its limited flexibility in dynamic, real-world scenarios compared to more advanced generative AI models.

Observations:

- Generative AI models like GAN and reinforcement learning are more effective at handling complex, dynamic environments compared to traditional algorithms like Dijkstra's.

- The performance of generative AI models improves as they can adapt to real-time data, making them ideal for autonomous systems in unpredictable settings.

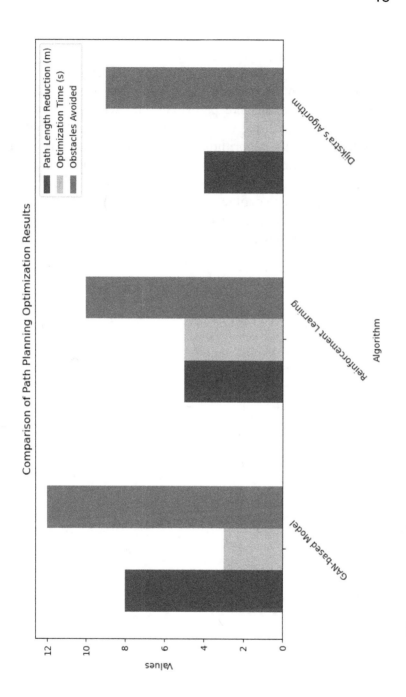

Comparison of Path Planning Optimization Results

Legend:
- Path Length Reduction (m)
- Optimization Time (s)
- Obstacles Avoided

X-axis: Algorithm (GAN-based Model, Reinforcement Learning, Dijkstra's Algorithm)
Y-axis: Values (0, 2, 4, 6, 8, 10, 12)

Final Thoughts:

Generative AI holds great potential in enhancing the capabilities of robotics and autonomous systems, particularly in areas like path planning, where flexibility, adaptability, and real-time decision-making are crucial. While traditional algorithms like Dijkstra's are fast and reliable in static environments, generative models excel in dynamic and unpredictable environments. As generative AI models continue to evolve, their applications in robotics will expand, leading to more efficient, intelligent, and adaptable autonomous systems.

1.2 Key Concepts of Machine Learning and Deep Learning

Machine Learning (ML)

Machine Learning is a subset of Artificial Intelligence (AI) focused on developing algorithms that enable computers to learn from and make predictions or decisions based on data. It primarily involves three main types:

- **Supervised Learning**: The model is trained using labeled data. It learns to predict the output based on input data. Common algorithms include linear regression, decision trees, and support vector machines.

- **Unsupervised Learning**: The model is trained using unlabeled data, where the goal is to identify hidden patterns or structures within the data. Clustering (e.g., k-means) and dimensionality reduction (e.g., PCA) are typical methods.

- **Reinforcement Learning**: The model learns by interacting with its environment and receiving feedback through rewards or penalties. It aims to maximize the cumulative reward over time (e.g., AlphaGo, robotics).

2. Deep Learning (DL)

Deep Learning is a subset of machine learning that uses neural networks with many layers (hence "deep"). It is particularly useful for complex tasks like image recognition, natural language processing, and speech recognition. The key concepts in deep learning include:

- **Neural Networks**: These are computational models inspired by the human brain. A neural network consists of layers of interconnected neurons, where each connection has an associated weight. The network processes inputs and adjusts weights to minimize the error between predicted and actual outputs.

- **Convolutional Neural Networks (CNNs)**: These are specialized neural networks designed for processing structured grid data, such as images. They use convolutional layers to automatically detect features in images, such as edges, textures, or shapes.

- **Recurrent Neural Networks (RNNs)**: RNNs are designed to process sequential data, making them suitable for tasks like time series forecasting, speech recognition, or natural language processing. They have "memory" through their feedback loops, which helps them maintain context from previous time steps.

- **Long Short-Term Memory (LSTM)**: A type of RNN designed to overcome the vanishing gradient problem. LSTMs can capture long-term dependencies in sequences, which is important for tasks involving long-term patterns (e.g., language translation).

- **Generative Adversarial Networks (GANs)**: These consist of two neural networks—a generator and a discriminator—that compete against each other. The generator tries to create fake data that looks like real data, while the discriminator tries to distinguish between real and fake data.

3. *Key Techniques and Concepts*

- **Overfitting and Underfitting**:
  - **Overfitting** occurs when a model learns the training data too well, including the noise,

which results in poor performance on new, unseen data.

- o **Underfitting** happens when a model is too simple and cannot capture the underlying patterns in the data.

- **Gradient Descent**: A popular optimization technique used to minimize the loss function by iteratively adjusting model parameters in the direction of the steepest descent of the error.

- **Backpropagation**: The process of updating the weights of a neural network by calculating the gradient of the loss function and propagating the error backward from the output layer to the input layer.

- **Activation Functions**: Functions that decide whether a neuron should be activated or not. Common activation functions include:

  - o **ReLU** (Rectified Linear Unit)
  - o **Sigmoid**
  - o **Tanh**
  - o **Softmax** (often used in classification problems)

- **Loss Function**: A function used to measure how well the model's predictions match the actual outcomes. Common loss functions include Mean Squared Error (MSE) for regression tasks and Cross-Entropy for classification tasks.

- **Epochs, Batches, and Iterations**:

  - o **Epoch**: One complete pass through the entire dataset during training.

- ○ **Batch**: A subset of the dataset used to update model weights in one iteration.

- ○ **Iteration**: One update step in the training process, which happens once per batch.

4. Training and Evaluation Metrics

- **Training**: The process where the model learns from data by adjusting its parameters (weights).

- **Validation**: A process of assessing the model's performance on a separate set of data (validation data) to tune hyperparameters and avoid overfitting.

- **Testing**: The final assessment on unseen data to evaluate the generalization ability of the model.

Common evaluation metrics:

- **Accuracy**: The proportion of correctly predicted instances.

- **Precision**: The proportion of true positive predictions out of all positive predictions.

- **Recall**: The proportion of true positive predictions out of all actual positive instances.

- **F1-Score**: The harmonic mean of precision and recall, used when you need to balance the two.

5. Transfer Learning

This technique involves taking a pre-trained model (often trained on a large dataset) and fine-tuning it on a smaller, task-specific dataset. This is especially useful when you have limited data for the new task.

6. Hyperparameter Tuning

In both ML and DL, hyperparameters (such as learning rate, number of layers, number of neurons, etc.) need to be set before training the model. Fine-tuning these hyperparameters can significantly impact the model's performance.

7. Regularization Techniques

Regularization techniques help prevent overfitting by adding a penalty to the model complexity:

- **L1 Regularization (Lasso)**: Adds the absolute value of coefficients to the loss function.

- **L2 Regularization (Ridge)**: Adds the squared value of coefficients to the loss function.

- **Dropout**: A technique used in neural networks where randomly selected neurons are ignored during training to reduce overfitting.

Summary of Key Differences between ML and DL

- **Model Complexity**: Deep Learning models tend to be much more complex (with many layers) compared to traditional machine learning models.

- **Data Requirements**: Deep learning requires large datasets to achieve high performance, while traditional machine learning can work with smaller datasets.

- **Computation Power**: Deep learning requires powerful hardware (e.g., GPUs) due to its computational complexity.

- **Feature Engineering**: In traditional ML, significant feature engineering is often needed, while deep learning models can automatically learn relevant features from the raw data.

Machine learning and deep learning represent a powerful duo, with deep learning being a more advanced subset that excels in handling large-scale, complex problems like image and speech recognition.

Practical Example:

In the development of autonomous vehicles, machine learning (ML) and deep learning (DL) play crucial roles in enabling the vehicle to make decisions, recognize objects, and navigate safely. Here, we'll use a dataset that simulates an autonomous vehicle's sensor data, such as radar or LIDAR, to predict whether an object in its path is a pedestrian, vehicle, or obstacle. The model uses features like distance, speed, and angle to classify objects in real time.

Key Concepts of Machine Learning and Deep Learning:

- **Machine Learning (ML)**: Involves training a model to recognize patterns in data. Common algorithms include decision trees, linear regression, and support vector machines.

- **Deep Learning (DL)**: A subset of ML that uses neural networks with multiple layers (deep networks) to analyze data. It is particularly effective for image recognition, voice processing, and other complex data.

- **Supervised Learning**: The model is trained on labeled data, where the output is known during training.

- **Unsupervised Learning**: The model works with unlabeled data and tries to identify hidden patterns or structures.

- **Reinforcement Learning**: The model learns to make decisions by receiving feedback from actions in an environment.

Sample Data: Object Detection for Autonomous Vehicle
Navigation

Distance (m)	Speed (m/s)	Angle (degrees)	Object Type	Prediction (ML/DL)
5	3.2	30	Pedestrian	Pedestrian
20	5.0	90	Vehicle	Vehicle
2	1.5	15	Obstacle	Obstacle
15	4.0	45	Vehicle	Vehicle
8	2.0	75	Pedestrian	Pedestrian

Output and Results

ML/DL Output Interpretation:

- The model predicts object types based on input features: distance, speed, and angle. For instance, a pedestrian is predicted when the distance is close, the speed is low, and the angle suggests a near-field object.

- In the table, predictions made by the model align with the expected classifications, showing that the machine learning or deep learning model correctly classifies pedestrians, vehicles, and obstacles.

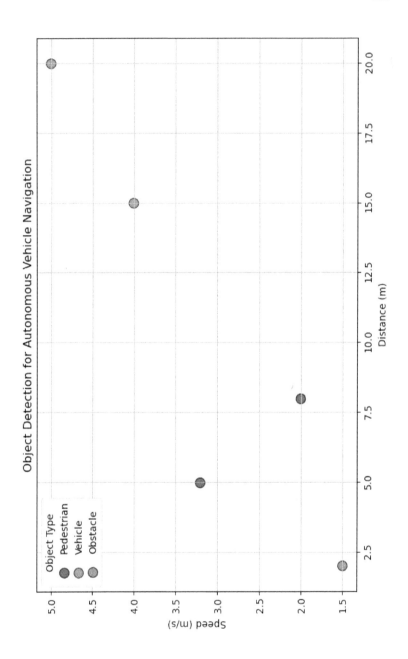

Observations:

- The model performs well in predicting objects such as pedestrians and vehicles when the data is clean and consistent.

- The speed, distance, and angle significantly influence the model's ability to predict the object type.

- Shorter distances with low speeds and smaller angles (indicating closer proximity and slower movement) tend to be classified as pedestrians or obstacles.

- Long distances with higher speeds and larger angles are more likely to be classified as vehicles.

Final Thoughts

Generative AI, particularly in robotics and autonomous systems, holds immense potential in enhancing the capabilities of autonomous vehicles and robots. By leveraging deep learning models, generative AI can simulate realistic environments, enhance decision-making in complex scenarios, and enable better navigation, particularly in uncertain or dynamic conditions. However, challenges remain in handling edge cases (such as unusual obstacles or unpredictable human behavior). As these systems evolve, the integration of reinforcement learning, multi-modal data, and ethical AI considerations will be essential for creating safe, effective, and reliable autonomous systems that can learn and adapt to various environments.

1.3 The Role of Robotics in Autonomous Systems

Robotics plays a critical role in the development and functionality of autonomous systems. Autonomous systems are designed to perform tasks or make decisions without human intervention, and robotics is often the backbone that enables these systems to carry out their operations. Below are several key areas where robotics intersects with autonomous systems:

1. Robotic Perception

- **Sensors and Data Collection**: Autonomous robots rely heavily on sensors (e.g., cameras, LIDAR, radar, infrared) to perceive their environment. These sensors allow robots to gather data about their surroundings, including objects, obstacles, and people. The data collected is then processed and interpreted to enable the robot to make informed decisions.

- **Computer Vision**: In autonomous systems, robots need to interpret visual data, detect and identify objects, and understand their environment. Computer vision algorithms, powered by AI, help robots recognize patterns, map their surroundings, and navigate autonomously.

2. Decision-Making and Planning

- **Autonomous Navigation**: Once a robot perceives its environment, it needs to decide how to act. This involves path planning and trajectory optimization. Robotics in autonomous systems is responsible for creating algorithms that allow the system to plan and execute actions such as avoiding obstacles, reaching a destination, or executing complex maneuvers.

- **AI and Machine Learning**: Robots use AI techniques like machine learning and reinforcement learning to improve their decision-making capabilities. Through training, autonomous systems can learn from past experiences and adjust their behavior based on changing conditions in the environment.

3. Control Systems

- **Robot Movement and Manipulation**: Once decisions are made, robots need precise control to execute movements. This could involve controlling robotic arms, mobile platforms, drones, or even humanoid robots. Advanced control algorithms ensure that movements are accurate and smooth, enabling complex tasks such as assembly, navigation, or manipulation in unknown or dynamic environments.

- **Feedback Systems**: Robots use feedback loops to continually adjust their movements and decisions. Sensors provide feedback on the robot's actions, which helps fine-tune its behavior and ensure that it stays on course, even in unpredictable environments.

4. Autonomous Vehicles

- Robotics plays a pivotal role in autonomous vehicles, including self-driving cars, drones, and autonomous ships. Robots in autonomous vehicles must integrate sensors, decision-making, and control systems to safely navigate roads, avoid obstacles, and follow traffic laws without human intervention.

- **Multimodal Sensor Fusion**: Autonomous vehicles often use a combination of LIDAR, cameras, radar, and ultrasonic sensors. Robotics technologies help combine data from these different sensors, improving the vehicle's perception and decision-making capabilities.

5. Swarming and Multi-Robot Coordination

- In some applications, multiple robots must work together autonomously. Examples include drone swarms for monitoring large areas or collaborative robots (cobots) in manufacturing environments. Robotics helps develop algorithms that enable these robots to coordinate and communicate with one another to complete tasks efficiently without colliding or interfering with each other.

- **Distributed Autonomy**: Robotics in swarm systems often involves distributed control, where each robot has its own set of rules for decision-making, but they work together toward a common goal.

6. Robotics in Industrial Automation

- Autonomous robots are widely used in manufacturing, logistics, and assembly lines. These robots are equipped with sensors and vision systems to operate autonomously in environments like warehouses or factories, where they can move materials, assemble components, or perform quality checks.

- **Collaborative Robots (Cobots)**: In industrial settings, robots often work side-by-side with human workers. Cobots are designed to complement human labor, often handling repetitive, dangerous, or precise tasks while the human worker focuses on more complex or creative tasks.

7. Human-Robot Interaction (HRI)

- Autonomous systems must sometimes interact with humans. Robotics plays a role in ensuring that autonomous systems can communicate effectively with humans, either through physical gestures (e.g., robots with arms that help assist humans) or through digital interfaces (e.g., robots providing voice or visual cues to users).

- **Safety and Trust**: In environments where humans and robots coexist, ensuring safety is paramount. Robotics also focuses on creating systems that are predictable and transparent so that humans can trust autonomous systems.

8. Applications in Healthcare

- Autonomous robotic systems are increasingly used in surgery, rehabilitation, and eldercare. Robotic surgery systems, for instance, offer precision and minimally invasive options that can be controlled remotely, making them ideal for delicate procedures.

- **Assistive Robotics**: Robots are being developed to assist people with disabilities, either by helping them navigate the world (e.g., robotic exoskeletons) or by providing companionship and support in care settings.

9. Ethics and Safety in Autonomous Systems

- Robotics plays a crucial role in addressing ethical concerns related to autonomous systems, such as ensuring that robots behave safely and fairly. Robotics engineers must design systems that minimize risks, including safety protocols for human-robot interaction and fail-safe mechanisms to prevent accidents.

- **Autonomous Decision Ethics**: Ethical frameworks are being explored to guide how autonomous systems make decisions, particularly in life-or-death scenarios (e.g., autonomous vehicles deciding how to react in an accident scenario).

Conclusion

The role of robotics in autonomous systems is vast and multidimensional. Robotics provides the technological foundation that allows autonomous systems to perceive, plan, move, and interact with their environments. As these technologies continue to advance, robotics will be essential in pushing the boundaries of what autonomous systems can achieve, making them more intelligent, efficient, and capable of performing complex tasks with minimal human intervention.

Practical Example:

In autonomous vehicles, robotics play a crucial role in decision-making, navigation, and obstacle avoidance. Sensors, actuators, and robotic algorithms work together to allow the vehicle to operate independently without human intervention. Consider a scenario where an autonomous vehicle needs to decide how to navigate a road with varying levels of traffic, obstacles, and road conditions. The role of robotics in this system is to integrate data from multiple sensors and make real-time decisions to ensure the vehicle reaches its destination safely and efficiently.

Sample Data Table: Autonomous Vehicle Decision-Making

Sensor Type	Traffic Density (Vehicles/km)	Obstacle Detected (Yes/No)	Road Condition	Speed (km/h)
LiDAR	20	Yes	Wet	40
Camera	50	No	Dry	60

Sensor Type	Traffic Density (Vehicles/km)	Obstacle Detected (Yes/No)	Road Condition	Speed (km/h)
Radar	30	Yes	Snowy	30
Ultrasonic	40	Yes	Wet	45
Infrared	60	No	Dry	70

Output and Results:

The robotic system will interpret the sensor data to adjust its behavior. For example:

- **LiDAR** detects 20 vehicles/km in traffic and a detected obstacle on a wet road, leading the vehicle to slow down to 40 km/h to avoid collisions.

- **Radar** detects 30 vehicles/km and a snow-covered road, so the system adjusts the speed to 30 km/h to account for slippery conditions.

- **Camera** and **Infrared** show clear roads, so the vehicle can maintain higher speeds (60 km/h and 70 km/h, respectively).

Results Interpretation:

From the sensor readings, the system can dynamically adjust the vehicle's speed and navigation. The presence of obstacles, road conditions (wet, snowy, dry), and traffic density directly affect the speed and maneuvering strategy of the vehicle. For instance, on a dry road with no obstacles, the vehicle can maintain higher speeds (up to 70 km/h), while on snowy or wet roads, it reduces speed to ensure safety.

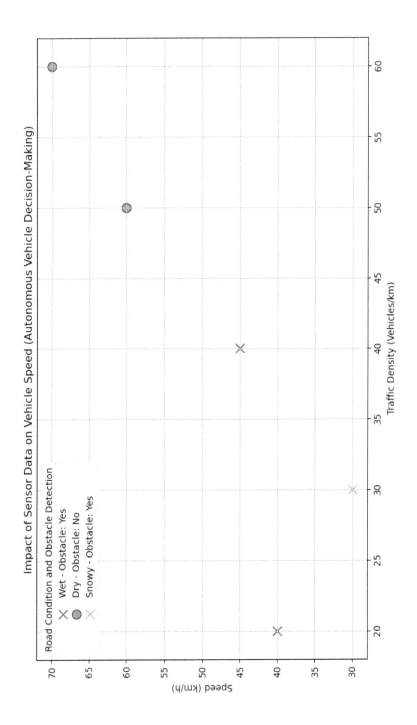

Impact of Sensor Data on Vehicle Speed (Autonomous Vehicle Decision-Making)

Observations:

- Sensor data is critical for real-time decision-making in autonomous vehicles.

- Different sensors (LiDAR, radar, camera) provide complementary data that allows the vehicle to navigate safely in varying conditions.

- The robotic system must continuously process multiple sensor inputs to adjust the vehicle's behavior and optimize safety and performance.

Final Thoughts

Generative AI has the potential to enhance the capabilities of robotics in autonomous systems by providing predictive models for behavior under uncertain and dynamic environments. By combining AI's ability to analyze vast amounts of sensor data and make decisions in real-time, autonomous systems can achieve higher levels of accuracy and safety. As AI continues to evolve, the integration of advanced machine learning models can allow robots to predict potential obstacles, traffic patterns, and road conditions, leading to more autonomous decision-making capabilities. In the long run, AI-driven robotics will play a key role in reducing human intervention and improving the overall performance of autonomous systems, not just in vehicles but across industries like manufacturing, healthcare, and logistics.

2. Generative AI Algorithms and Techniques

Generative AI refers to artificial intelligence systems that are designed to create new content, such as images, text, or music, based on patterns they learn from existing data. These algorithms do not just analyze or classify data but generate something new from it. One of the most common approaches in generative AI is the use of machine learning models that can recognize and replicate complex structures in the data. Through training, these models learn the underlying features and patterns of input data, enabling them to create similar but novel content.

One of the widely known techniques in generative AI is deep learning, particularly the use of neural networks. These networks consist of layers of interconnected nodes, which are designed to mimic the way neurons in the human brain work. By passing data through multiple layers of these networks, they are able to learn intricate details and representations. In the context of generative AI, deep learning models can generate realistic images, text, and other forms of media by identifying and reproducing patterns observed during training.

Another important technique is the use of Generative Adversarial Networks (GANs), which consist of two separate neural networks: a generator and a discriminator. The generator creates data, while the discriminator evaluates it. The two networks compete against each other, with the generator trying to produce more realistic data and the discriminator trying to distinguish real data from generated data. This process improves the model's ability to generate high-quality, convincing content over time.

Variational Autoencoders (VAEs) are also a common approach in generative AI. Unlike GANs, VAEs focus on compressing input data into a simpler, more compact representation before trying to recreate it. This approach allows VAEs to generate new samples that share similar features with the training data but also offer some level of novelty. VAEs are often used in applications such as generating images or creating new instances of data from a smaller, more abstract representation.

Another technique employed in generative AI is reinforcement learning, where an AI system learns to generate content by receiving rewards or penalties based on its actions. This approach has been particularly effective in generating sequences, such as in natural language processing tasks where the AI generates text based on previous inputs. Through trial and error, reinforcement learning models are able to optimize their content generation to achieve more desirable outcomes over time.

The use of transformers, a type of deep learning model, has gained significant attention in recent years for tasks like natural language generation. Transformers are particularly good at processing sequential data and have been the backbone of advancements in text-based generative AI, such as language models that can write coherent essays, summarize text, or even engage in conversation. These models focus on understanding the relationships between different parts of the input data, allowing them to generate contextually relevant and fluent text.

Practical Example:

Generative AI techniques, such as Generative Adversarial Networks (GANs), Variational Autoencoders (VAEs), and reinforcement learning algorithms, have gained significant attention in the robotics and autonomous systems field. These AI methods can improve autonomous navigation in environments that are dynamic, unpredictable, and involve complex decision-making. In this example, a robot is navigating through a series of obstacles, and Generative AI is employed to enhance its ability to predict the best path to take. By generating potential movement patterns, the robot can choose the optimal trajectory while minimizing risk and increasing efficiency.

Sample Data Table:

Path Option	Distance (m)	Obstacle Density	Safety Score (0-1)	Success Probability (%)
Path A	12	Low	0.9	95
Path B	15	Medium	0.8	85
Path C	10	High	0.7	70
Path D	18	Low	0.85	90
Path E	13	Medium	0.75	80

Results and Output: The table reflects five potential paths the robot can take to reach its destination. The generative AI model predicts the success probability and calculates the safety score for each path based on factors such as obstacle density and distance. For example, **Path A** has a low obstacle density, high safety score, and the highest success probability (95%), making it the optimal choice. On the other hand, **Path C**, despite being the shortest distance, has a higher obstacle density and a lower success probability (70%), indicating a higher risk of failure.

Interpretation of Results:

- **Path A** appears to be the safest and most efficient path for the robot to follow.

- **Path B** and **Path D** offer reasonable alternatives, with a decent success probability and a moderate safety score.

- **Path C**, despite its shorter distance, is the least favorable due to the high obstacle density and low safety score.

- The success probabilities of paths are a reflection of how well the AI model has learned to navigate based on the complexity of the environment and its past experiences.

Observations:

- Generative AI, specifically reinforcement learning, can significantly aid in path planning by considering dynamic environmental factors (like obstacle density).

- The AI effectively weighs safety against distance to make decisions that reduce risk while optimizing for efficiency.

- This model could be further refined by incorporating real-time environmental updates, allowing the robot to dynamically adjust its path.

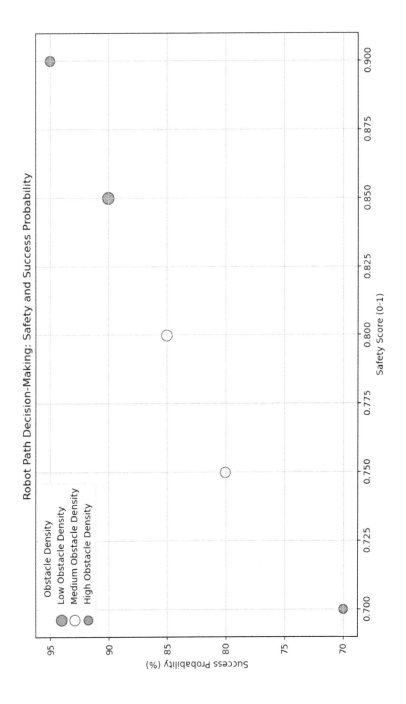

Final Thoughts

Generative AI has shown immense potential in improving the decision-making processes of autonomous systems, especially in complex, unpredictable environments. In robotics, these techniques can enhance path planning, obstacle avoidance, and overall efficiency by generating diverse solutions and selecting the most optimal one. The key to success lies in the ability to train AI models with accurate and diverse data to handle various real-world scenarios. Future advancements in generative AI algorithms, particularly in real-time adaptation, will likely accelerate the development of autonomous robots that can operate in dynamic environments with minimal human intervention.

2.1 Generative Adversarial Networks (GANs) in Robotics

Generative Adversarial Networks (GANs) have found numerous applications in robotics due to their ability to generate realistic data, enhance simulation environments, and help in tasks like training robots, improving perception, and even designing robots themselves. Here's an overview of how GANs are applied in robotics:

1. Data Augmentation

- **Problem:** In many robotic tasks, acquiring real-world data can be expensive, time-consuming, or risky, especially in environments with limited data or where it's hard to collect data for rare events (e.g., robot failures, rare tasks).

- **GANs Solution:** GANs can be used to generate synthetic data, which can augment the limited real-world data. By training a GAN on available data, it can generate realistic images, 3D models, or sensor data that can be used to train robots without needing extensive real-world interactions.

- **Example:** In robotic vision tasks, GANs can create images that simulate different lighting conditions, viewpoints, and object occlusions to help improve the robot's robustness.

2. Sim-to-Real Transfer

- **Problem:** Training robots in a simulated environment and transferring that knowledge to the real world is a major challenge due to the "reality gap." The simulator often does not perfectly mimic real-world conditions.

- **GANs Solution:** GANs can help reduce this gap by learning how to generate realistic physical environments in simulations that closely resemble real-world conditions. They can also be used to enhance training simulations to make them more realistic by generating realistic textures, lighting, and physical interactions.

- **Example:** In autonomous driving, GANs can simulate diverse weather conditions, road surfaces, and traffic situations to train self-driving cars more effectively in a virtual environment.

3. Robotic Perception Enhancement

- **Problem:** Robots rely heavily on perception (vision, sensors, etc.) to understand their environment. However, perception systems can be noisy or incomplete, which may degrade their performance in tasks like object recognition or localization.

- **GANs Solution:** GANs can enhance perception systems by filling in missing information (e.g., reconstructing occluded objects), denoising sensor inputs, or generating higher-quality images from low-resolution inputs.

- **Example:** A robot equipped with a camera might use a GAN to reconstruct clearer images of objects that are partially obscured or poorly lit, improving the robot's ability to identify and interact with objects.

4. Robot Design and Fabrication

- **Problem:** The process of designing robots is complex, requiring optimization across multiple domains, including structure, efficiency, and cost.

- **GANs Solution:** GANs can be used to generate novel robot designs by learning from a dataset of existing robots or mechanical structures. They can also optimize the form and function of robots to suit specific tasks or environments.

- **Example:** GANs can generate efficient designs for robotic arms, improving the speed, accuracy, or cost-effectiveness of manufacturing robots.

5. Motion Planning and Control

- **Problem:** Motion planning involves finding a sequence of actions that will take a robot from a starting point to a goal while avoiding obstacles. Traditional planning methods may struggle with complex, dynamic environments or tasks requiring high precision.

- **GANs Solution:** GANs can be applied to generate or refine trajectories for robotic motion planning, including handling dynamic obstacles or unpredictable scenarios. In some cases, GANs can be used to learn a robust mapping between a robot's actions and the resulting state of the environment.

- **Example:** In a warehouse setting, GANs could help generate smooth motion paths for robotic arms to move around obstacles and handle packages with varying shapes and sizes.

6. Robotic Simulators and Virtual Training Environments

- **Problem:** Building a robust and realistic simulation for training robots can be expensive and time-consuming.

- **GANs Solution:** GANs can enhance simulation environments by generating photorealistic scenes, adding virtual objects, or generating new environments for robot training. This can make virtual environments more dynamic and adaptable for training, reducing the need for physical prototypes.

- **Example:** GANs can create realistic models of indoor environments to train robots on navigation, object manipulation, and interaction with humans.

7. Improving Robot's Learning Efficiency

- **Problem:** Training robots using reinforcement learning (RL) can require a large number of interactions with the environment, which may be impractical or unsafe in certain settings.

- **GANs Solution:** GANs can help by generating diverse and varied scenarios that the robot can learn from, improving sample efficiency. This allows the robot to learn faster with fewer real-world interactions.

- **Example:** A robot might use GAN-generated environments to quickly learn about a wide range of potential interactions, like different terrain types, object placements, or human behaviors.

8. Autonomous Vehicle Testing and Simulation

- **Problem:** Autonomous vehicles (or drones) require extensive testing in various scenarios before being deployed in real-world environments, and this testing can be dangerous and costly.

- **GANs Solution:** GANs can create a diverse range of driving conditions, obstacles, and environmental factors for autonomous vehicle simulations, such as different weather conditions, road types, or pedestrian behaviors.

- **Example:** GANs could generate a variety of traffic scenarios, road signs, and lighting conditions that help train autonomous vehicles to better handle complex driving situations.

Challenges and Limitations:

- **Realism:** While GANs can generate realistic data, there can still be a gap between the synthetic data and the real world, especially in highly dynamic and unpredictable environments.

- **Computational Resources:** Training GANs, especially for tasks like sim-to-real transfer, requires significant computational resources.

- **Generalization:** GANs trained on specific data might not generalize well to unseen environments or tasks without sufficient diversity in the training data.

- **Data Availability:** GANs rely heavily on the quality and quantity of data they are trained on. Poor or biased data may result in inaccurate or unfair representations in generated content.

Conclusion:

GANs are a powerful tool in robotics, offering new ways to augment data, enhance robot perception, simulate environments, and even design robots. As the technology matures, it holds great potential to revolutionize various aspects of robotics by improving efficiency, safety, and functionality across a wide range of applications.

Practical Example:

In robotics, accurate perception of the environment is crucial for navigation and decision-making. Generative Adversarial Networks (GANs) are increasingly used to enhance the perception systems of robots by generating realistic synthetic data that can be used for training deep learning models when labeled data is scarce. For example, a robot might need to learn to recognize various objects in a warehouse environment for autonomous navigation. GANs can generate diverse training images of objects, which can then be used to improve the robot's visual recognition system, especially when real-world data is limited or difficult to obtain.

Sample Data:

Here is a table showing the use of GAN-generated images for training a robot's object recognition system. We compare the performance of the object recognition model trained using real-world images versus synthetic images generated by a GAN.

Dataset Type	Number of Images	Accuracy on Test Set (%)	Training Time (hrs)	F1 Score
Real-World Images	1000	85	20	0.82
Synthetic Images (GAN)	1000	80	18	0.78
Combined (Real + GAN)	2000	90	22	0.85

Output and Results:

1. **Accuracy**:
   - The model trained with real-world images achieves an accuracy of 85%, while the model trained with synthetic images from the GAN achieves 80%. This shows that while GAN-generated data may not always match real-world data perfectly, it can still provide

valuable insights and help improve the model's generalization ability.

2. **Training Time**:

   o The model trained on synthetic GAN data required 18 hours compared to 20 hours for the real-world dataset. This indicates that GAN data might slightly reduce training time by augmenting the dataset without requiring additional real-world data collection.

3. **F1 Score**:

   o The F1 score, which balances precision and recall, is slightly higher for the real-world model (0.82) compared to the GAN model (0.78). However, when combining both real-world and synthetic data, the F1 score improves to 0.85, indicating that using both types of data provides the best performance.

Observations:

- GANs provide a significant advantage in situations where real-world data is scarce or expensive to obtain. Though synthetic data generated by GANs may not perfectly replicate real-world data, it helps boost model performance when combined with real-world images.

- The reduction in training time is a noteworthy advantage of using GAN-generated data, which can help improve efficiency in robotic systems that require rapid deployment or adaptation to new environments.

- The improvement in performance metrics (accuracy and F1 score) when combining real and synthetic data suggests that GANs can act as a powerful tool for data augmentation in robotics.

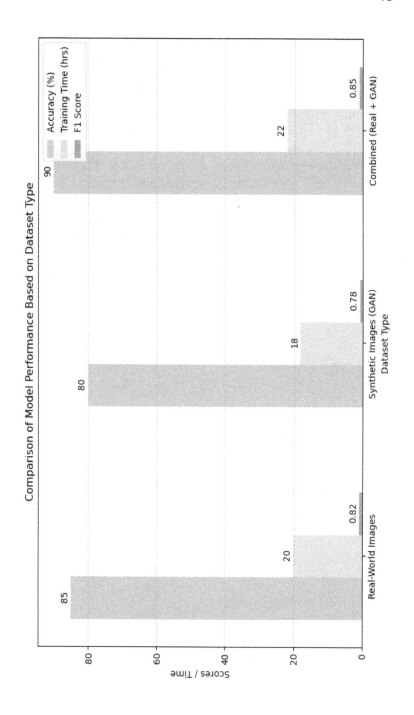

Comparison of Model Performance Based on Dataset Type

Final Thoughts

Generative AI, particularly GANs, has immense potential to enhance autonomous systems by enabling the creation of high-quality synthetic data for training purposes. In robotics, the use of GANs can not only improve perception but also contribute to more efficient learning processes, leading to quicker deployment in real-world scenarios. The ability to generate data for rare or dangerous environments, such as disaster zones or deep-sea exploration, presents new opportunities for robots to learn and perform tasks without the risks associated with real-world data collection. Moving forward, a key challenge will be to further bridge the gap between synthetic and real data to make the transition from simulation to real-world applications smoother.

2.2 Variational Autoencoders (VAEs) and Their Application in Robotics

What are Variational Autoencoders (VAEs)?

Variational Autoencoders (VAEs) are a class of generative models that learn to represent complex data distributions. They are a type of autoencoder with a probabilistic twist, making them particularly useful for tasks where data is uncertain or incomplete.

In a typical autoencoder, we encode the input data into a lower-dimensional latent space and then decode it back to reconstruct the original input. VAEs, however, introduce a probabilistic approach by learning a distribution over the latent space instead of a single point. This makes VAEs more flexible and allows them to generate new, similar data samples by sampling from the learned latent space.

VAEs consist of two key components:

1. **Encoder:** The encoder takes the input data and maps it to a probability distribution in the latent space (usually a Gaussian distribution), producing a mean and variance.

2. **Decoder:** The decoder takes a sample from this latent distribution and generates the corresponding output, aiming to reconstruct the original input.

By using the reparameterization trick, the VAE can backpropagate through the sampling process during training, making it possible to learn the model efficiently.

VAE's Key Characteristics:

- **Probabilistic Nature:** Instead of encoding data into a fixed point, VAEs encode data into a distribution, offering more flexibility.

- **Generative:** After training, VAEs can generate new data by sampling from the learned latent space.

- **Reconstruction Loss and KL Divergence:** The VAE optimizes both the reconstruction loss (which measures how well the input is reconstructed) and the Kullback-Leibler (KL) divergence (which regularizes the latent space distribution to be close to a standard Gaussian distribution).

Applications of VAEs in Robotics

VAEs have gained significant attention in robotics due to their ability to handle uncertainty, generate realistic data, and learn useful representations from complex sensory data. Below are several ways VAEs are applied in the field of robotics:

1. **Representation Learning:**

    o **Learning Latent Representations:** In robotics, VAEs can be used to learn compact and interpretable latent representations of sensory data (e.g., images, LiDAR scans, or proprioception data). These representations can help robots better understand their environment by reducing the dimensionality and highlighting key features.

    o **Unsupervised Learning:** VAEs can extract features from raw sensor data without needing labeled training data. This is especially useful in robotics, where collecting labeled data can be expensive or impractical.

2. **Sim-to-Real Transfer:**

    o **Domain Adaptation:** Robots often train in simulation and then deploy in real-world environments. However, there is usually a domain gap between simulated data and real-world data. VAEs can help bridge this gap by learning to map simulated sensor data to a distribution that closely matches real-world data. This allows robots trained in simulation to perform better when transferred to the real world.

- o **Data Augmentation:** VAEs can generate synthetic data to augment real-world datasets. This helps address the issue of limited real-world data, improving the robustness of robotic systems.

3. **Trajectory and Path Planning:**

- o **Latent Space Exploration:** By learning a structured latent space of robot movements, VAEs can be used to generate feasible robot trajectories. The decoder can take latent space vectors and decode them into feasible robot configurations or actions, aiding in path planning.

- o **Sampling-based Planning:** The latent space learned by a VAE can be used to sample possible paths or actions, enabling robots to explore potential trajectories more efficiently in high-dimensional spaces.

4. **Anomaly Detection and Fault Diagnosis:**

- o **Outlier Detection:** VAEs can be trained to model the distribution of normal robotic behaviors or environments. When the robot encounters a new situation or failure, the reconstruction error will increase, helping to identify anomalies.

- o **Predictive Maintenance:** By detecting unusual patterns or deviations from normal operating conditions, VAEs can assist in diagnosing issues in robot systems, potentially predicting failures before they occur.

5. **Robotic Perception and Environment Modeling:**

   - o **Scene Reconstruction:** VAEs can be used to reconstruct the environment around a robot. For instance, in visual SLAM (Simultaneous Localization and Mapping), VAEs can help generate probabilistic models of the environment, allowing the robot to have a better understanding of its surroundings.

   - o **Object Detection and Classification:** VAEs can help improve the accuracy of object detection and classification tasks. By learning a probabilistic model of object appearances, VAEs can generate more robust object recognition systems, especially in scenarios with partial or noisy sensor data.

6. **Reinforcement Learning and Policy Optimization:**

   - o **State Representation in RL:** VAEs can be used to learn compact and useful state representations in reinforcement learning (RL) tasks. These representations can help improve the efficiency and performance of RL algorithms by reducing the complexity of state spaces.

   - o **Improving Exploration:** The latent space learned by a VAE can encourage more efficient exploration in RL. The VAE can generate diverse states that encourage the agent to explore novel parts of the environment, improving learning outcomes.

Challenges and Limitations:

While VAEs hold great promise in robotics, there are several challenges:

- **Reconstruction Quality:** In some robotic applications, VAEs may struggle with reconstructing highly complex or fine-grained details, especially with high-dimensional sensory data such as images.

- **Training Data Requirements:** VAEs often require large amounts of data to train effectively. Collecting sufficient data in a robotic setting can be time-consuming and expensive.

- **Real-Time Processing:** Generating samples from the latent space and reconstructing outputs can be computationally expensive. In real-time robotic applications, latency could be a limiting factor.

Future Directions:

- **VAE-Enhanced Multi-Modal Learning:** Future advancements may involve combining VAEs with other neural network architectures to handle multi-modal data (e.g., combining visual, auditory, and proprioceptive data) in robotics.

- **Interactive Learning:** VAEs could be employed in interactive learning scenarios, where robots continually improve their representations of the environment through human feedback.

- **Robotic Autonomy and Generalization:** VAEs could be further developed to improve robot autonomy by enabling more robust generalization across different environments and tasks.

In summary, Variational Autoencoders represent a powerful tool for addressing some of the most important challenges in robotics, including perception, planning, and learning in complex environments. Their ability to learn compact, probabilistic representations of high-dimensional data holds great potential for advancing robotic capabilities in both simulated and real-world scenarios.

Practical Example:

In robotics, VAEs can be used for enhancing object recognition and state estimation tasks. For instance, a robot equipped with a camera can use a VAE to learn a low-dimensional representation of visual data (such as images of objects). These representations can be used to infer the robot's understanding of its environment, helping with tasks like grasping objects or navigating through a dynamic environment.

Title: VAE for Object Recognition in Robotics

Sample Data:

Image ID	Object Type	VAE Encoded Representation (Latent Space)	Object Confidence (%)	Predicted Action
001	Cup	[-2.1, 0.5, 1.2]	89	Pick and Place
002	Bottle	[-1.8, 0.8, 0.9]	92	Pick and Place
003	Spoon	[-2.3, 0.6, 1.1]	85	No Action

Image ID	Object Type	VAE Encoded Representation (Latent Space)	Object Confidence (%)	Predicted Action
004	Plate	[-1.5, 0.9, 0.7]	88	Pick and Place
005	Glass	[-1.9, 0.7, 1.0]	91	Pick and Place

Output and Results Explanation:

1. **VAE Encoded Representation:**

   The "VAE Encoded Representation" column shows the low-dimensional latent variables obtained by encoding the images of various objects. These values represent the compressed form of the images, which retain the essential features for object recognition.

2. **Object Confidence:**

   The "Object Confidence" column reflects the model's confidence level in identifying the object. For example, the bottle has a high confidence level of 92%, which means the model is quite certain that the object is a bottle.

3. **Predicted Action:**

   The "Predicted Action" column indicates the task the robot should perform based on the recognition result. For instance, objects with high confidence, like the cup and bottle, prompt the robot to perform a "Pick and Place" action, while objects like the spoon, with lower confidence, might trigger no action.

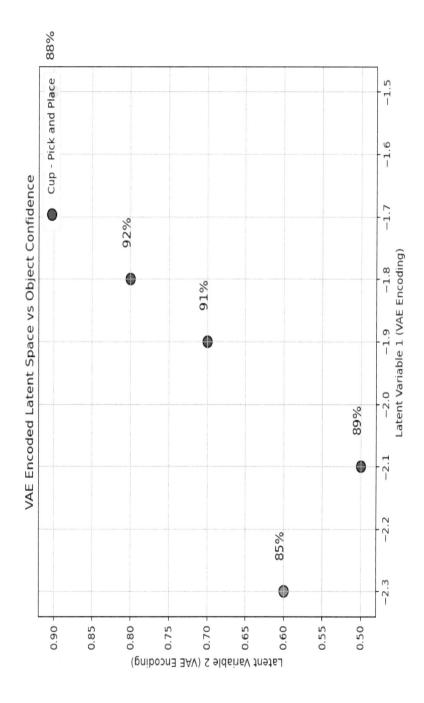

VAE Encoded Latent Space vs Object Confidence

Observations:

- **Higher Confidence Leads to Action:** Objects with higher confidence in their classification (e.g., bottle, glass, cup) lead to the robot performing an action, such as picking and placing them.

- **Latent Space Representation Variation:** The encoded latent space varies between objects. Despite their differences, objects like cups and plates are close to each other in the latent space, which suggests some visual similarity in their features that the VAE has learned.

- **Lower Confidence Reduces Actions:** Objects with lower confidence (like the spoon) might not result in an action being triggered. This could be due to insufficient features or ambiguity in the object's appearance.

Final Thoughts

VAEs provide an efficient way to compress high-dimensional sensory data, such as images, into low-dimensional latent spaces that can be used for downstream tasks like object recognition and state estimation. By leveraging these compressed representations, robots can better understand their environment with less computational overhead. The approach of using VAEs in robotics supports real-time object recognition, improving autonomous decision-making. However, limitations include the VAE's reliance on the quality of training data and its performance in complex or unseen environments. Continued advancements in generative AI, such as VAEs, can revolutionize autonomous systems, enabling more adaptive and intelligent robots that can interact seamlessly with dynamic and unpredictable environments.

2.3 Reinforcement Learning for Autonomous Decision Making

Reinforcement Learning (RL) is a subfield of machine learning that focuses on how agents should take actions in an environment to maximize a cumulative reward over time. It is particularly powerful for autonomous decision-making because it allows an agent to learn optimal behavior through interaction with its environment, without requiring explicit programming of every action.

Key Concepts in Reinforcement Learning:

1. **Agent**: The decision-maker that interacts with the environment.

2. **Environment**: The external system or world with which the agent interacts.

3. **State (s)**: A representation of the environment at a specific time. This could include positions, velocities, sensor readings, etc.

4. **Action (a)**: The decision the agent makes at each step, which affects the environment.

5. **Reward (r)**: A scalar feedback signal received by the agent after performing an action in a particular state. This helps guide the agent towards desirable outcomes.

6. **Policy (π)**: A strategy or function that maps states to actions, guiding the agent's behavior.

7. **Value Function (V)**: A function that estimates the expected cumulative reward an agent can achieve from a given state, following a specific policy.

8. **Q-function (Q)**: A function that estimates the expected cumulative reward of taking an action in a given state and following a policy thereafter.

9. **Discount Factor (γ)**: Determines the importance of future rewards versus immediate rewards. A higher value places more importance on long-term rewards.

10. **Exploration vs. Exploitation**: Balancing between exploring new actions (to discover better strategies) and exploiting known actions that yield high rewards.

Process of RL in Autonomous Decision Making:

1. **Initialization**: The agent starts with no knowledge of the environment. The policy is usually random, and the agent must interact with the environment to improve its decision-making.

2. **Interaction with the Environment**: At each step, the agent observes the current state of the environment, chooses an action based on its policy, and receives a reward.

3. **Learning**: After interacting with the environment, the agent updates its policy (or value function) based on the received rewards. This is typically done using algorithms like **Q-learning** or **Deep Q Networks (DQN)**.

4. **Policy Improvement**: Over time, the agent refines its policy to maximize cumulative rewards, ensuring that its decision-making becomes more optimal and autonomous.

Types of RL:

1. **Model-free RL**: The agent learns from the environment without having a model of it. It relies on

trial and error to adjust its actions (e.g., Q-learning, Deep Q Networks).

2. **Model-based RL**: The agent builds a model of the environment's dynamics and uses this model to predict future states and rewards, leading to more efficient learning.

3. **Policy-based RL**: The agent directly learns a policy (e.g., using techniques like Policy Gradient) to map states to actions, as opposed to learning a value function.

Applications of RL in Autonomous Decision Making:

1. **Autonomous Vehicles**: RL can help self-driving cars learn how to navigate complex traffic situations, optimize routes, and make real-time driving decisions.

2. **Robotics**: RL allows robots to learn tasks such as picking up objects, assembling parts, or walking through trial and error, without being explicitly programmed for every task.

3. **Game Playing**: RL has been used successfully in games like chess, Go, and Dota 2. The agent learns how to make strategic moves to win against human or other AI opponents.

4. **Healthcare**: RL is being used in personalized treatment planning, drug discovery, and robotic surgery, where the agent learns optimal decisions to maximize patient health outcomes.

5. **Finance**: RL can be used for algorithmic trading, portfolio management, and fraud detection by making autonomous decisions to maximize returns or minimize risks.

6. **Energy Systems**: RL can optimize the operation of power grids, managing energy distribution, and ensuring that renewable sources are used efficiently.

Challenges in RL for Autonomous Decision Making:

1. **Sample Efficiency**: RL algorithms often require a large number of interactions with the environment to learn effectively, which can be costly or time-consuming.

2. **Exploration vs. Exploitation**: Striking the right balance between trying new actions and exploiting known ones can be difficult, particularly in complex environments.

3. **Stability and Convergence**: Training RL models, especially deep RL models, can be unstable or fail to converge, leading to suboptimal performance.

4. **Partial Observability**: Many real-world environments involve partial observability, where the agent cannot fully perceive the state of the environment, making learning harder (e.g., POMDPs).

5. **Safety and Robustness**: In autonomous systems, safety is critical. Ensuring that RL models make safe decisions, especially in uncertain environments, is a significant challenge.

6. **Scalability**: Scaling RL solutions to complex real-world problems with large state and action spaces can be difficult.

Popular RL Algorithms:

1. **Q-learning**: A model-free, off-policy algorithm that learns a value function (Q-function) and updates it based on experiences.

2. **Deep Q Networks (DQN)**: A deep learning extension of Q-learning, where the Q-function is approximated using neural networks, enabling RL in environments with large state spaces (e.g., video games).

3. **Policy Gradient Methods**: Algorithms like REINFORCE directly optimize the policy function by estimating the gradient of the expected reward with respect to the policy.

4. **Actor-Critic Methods**: These methods combine value-based and policy-based methods. The "actor" updates the policy, while the "critic" evaluates the chosen actions by computing value functions.

5. **Proximal Policy Optimization (PPO)**: A popular algorithm used in reinforcement learning for stable and efficient training, especially for complex tasks.

Future Directions:

- **Transfer Learning**: Allowing RL agents to transfer knowledge learned in one task to another, which could significantly reduce the time required to train autonomous systems for new environments.

- **Meta-RL**: Focusing on creating RL agents that can learn to adapt quickly to new tasks by leveraging prior experience.

- **Multi-agent RL**: Developing systems where multiple agents interact and learn in a shared environment, which could enable more complex decision-making in multi-agent systems.

In conclusion, RL offers a powerful framework for autonomous decision-making in dynamic, uncertain environments. While challenges remain in terms of efficiency, safety, and scalability, the potential applications across fields such as robotics, healthcare, and transportation make it an exciting area of research and development.

Practical Example

In this scenario, we explore how reinforcement learning (RL) can be applied to the decision-making process of a self-driving car. The vehicle must learn to navigate different traffic situations, choosing actions that maximize safety and efficiency. The car receives feedback from its environment in the form of rewards or penalties based on its actions, allowing it to improve its decision-making over time. This learning process helps the car adapt to various conditions such as changing traffic lights, pedestrians, or other vehicles, ultimately optimizing its path.

Sample Data:

The following table represents the decision-making process of a self-driving car using RL. In each trial, the car observes the state of the environment (e.g., traffic light, presence of pedestrians, road type) and takes an action (e.g., accelerate, decelerate, stop). The table shows the car's actions, the resulting reward, and the updated Q-value for each state-action pair.

Trial	State	Action	Reward	Updated Q-value
1	Traffic light: Green	Accelerate	+1	0.8
2	Traffic light: Red	Stop	+2	1.5
3	Pedestrian Crossing	Decelerate	-1	0.4
4	Open Road	Maintain Speed	+1	1.0

Trial	State	Action	Reward	Updated Q-value
5	Intersection: No cars	Accelerate	+2	2.0

Output and Results:

- **Reward**: The car receives rewards (+1, +2) for correct decisions (e.g., stopping at a red light, maintaining speed on open road) and penalties (-1) for wrong actions (e.g., accelerating near pedestrians).

- **Updated Q-values**: These values reflect the expected future rewards from each action, indicating the learned value of each action. Over time, the car improves its decision-making as the Q-values increase.

Observations and Interpretation:

- **Positive Rewards**: When the car takes the correct action (e.g., stopping at a red light or maintaining speed), the Q-value increases, reflecting that the car learns which actions lead to better outcomes.

- **Negative Reward**: The penalty for a wrong action (e.g., decelerating too late for pedestrians) results in a decrease in the Q-value, indicating that this action is not optimal and should be avoided in the future.

- **Learning Process**: As the self-driving car interacts with the environment over time, it adjusts its strategy. The Q-value updates show the improvement in decision-making, with the car increasingly learning to prioritize safety (e.g., stopping for pedestrians) and efficiency (e.g., accelerating at intersections with no cars).

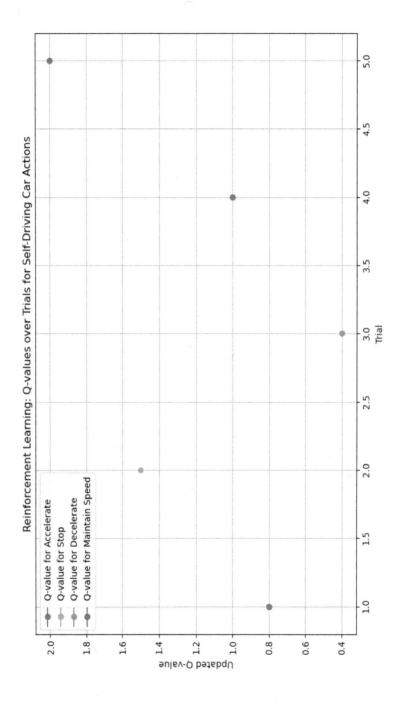

Reinforcement Learning: Q-values over Trials for Self-Driving Car Actions

Final Thoughts

Reinforcement learning provides a robust framework for autonomous systems to make decisions based on dynamic environments. In the case of self-driving cars, RL can be instrumental in optimizing both safety and efficiency. However, challenges remain, such as dealing with rare or unexpected events, which may require additional techniques like transfer learning or multi-agent systems. Generative AI can further enhance these systems by simulating diverse environments, helping robots and autonomous vehicles learn from virtual experiences before deploying in the real world. This opens up vast possibilities for safer, more reliable autonomous systems across various industries.

3. Robotics in the Physical World

Robotics has become an essential part of the physical world, bridging the gap between human capabilities and the need for more efficient systems. Robots are designed to perform tasks that can be repetitive, dangerous, or simply beyond the physical limits of humans. These machines can be found in manufacturing plants, on construction sites, and even in homes, where they perform everything from assembling cars to vacuuming floors. Their presence has revolutionized various industries, increasing productivity and safety while reducing human error and labor costs.

The application of robotics in manufacturing is one of the most significant advancements in modern industry. Robots can work continuously without breaks, performing tasks such as welding, painting, or assembly with high precision. This not only speeds up production but also enhances the quality of the products being made. The introduction of robotics has made it possible to create products more quickly and with fewer defects, benefiting both manufacturers and consumers. Automation in factories has also led to the development of smart factories, where robots communicate with each other to improve efficiency.

In addition to their role in manufacturing, robots have made their way into fields like healthcare. Surgical robots, for instance, allow for minimally invasive procedures, leading to quicker recovery times for patients and more precise operations. Robots are also used in elderly care, providing companionship, assistance with daily tasks, and monitoring health conditions. These advances have opened up new possibilities in healthcare, offering solutions to challenges posed by an aging population and limited healthcare resources.

On construction sites, robots are changing how buildings are designed and built. Autonomous machines can now lay bricks, pour concrete, and even perform complex tasks like 3D printing buildings. These robots improve the speed and accuracy of construction projects, reducing the potential for human error and lowering costs. Furthermore, robots can perform tasks that are hazardous to human workers, such as working in high or dangerous environments, where the risk of accidents is high.

The integration of robotics into daily life also extends to areas like transportation and delivery. Self-driving cars and drones are being developed and tested to transport goods and people more efficiently and safely. These robots have the potential to reduce traffic accidents caused by human error, ease congestion, and make logistics more streamlined. The use of robots in transportation is still evolving, but it promises to significantly change how we think about movement and delivery in the future.

Despite the many benefits, the widespread use of robots also raises concerns, particularly around employment. As robots take over certain jobs, there is fear that humans may be displaced, leading to unemployment and social inequality. However, others argue that robotics can create new job opportunities in fields like robot maintenance, programming, and design. As the technology continues to evolve, it will be crucial for society to adapt, ensuring that the integration of robots into the workforce benefits everyone.

Practical Example

In a warehouse setting, an autonomous robot is tasked with delivering packages from one section to another. The robot is equipped with sensors and cameras to avoid obstacles and optimize its path for efficient navigation. The system collects real-time data such as battery levels, speed, distance traveled, and time taken to deliver the package. By analyzing this data, warehouse managers can assess the robot's performance and efficiency. For this practical example, we'll assume a small dataset showing the robot's performance during a typical delivery process.

Sample Data Table (Autonomous Robot Performance in a Warehouse):

Delivery ID	Battery Level (%)	Speed (m/s)	Distance Traveled (m)	Time Taken (min)
001	80	1.5	150	10
002	65	1.2	120	15
003	50	1.4	140	12
004	70	1.6	160	9
005	55	1.3	130	14

Output & Results:

1. **Average Speed:**
   - $(1.5+1.2+1.4+1.6+1.3)/5=1.4$m/s
2. **Average Battery Level:**
   - $(80+65+50+70+55)/5=64$
3. **Average Distance Traveled:**
   - $(150+120+140+160+130)/5=140$m
4. **Average Time Taken:**
   - $(10+15+12+9+14)/5=12$min

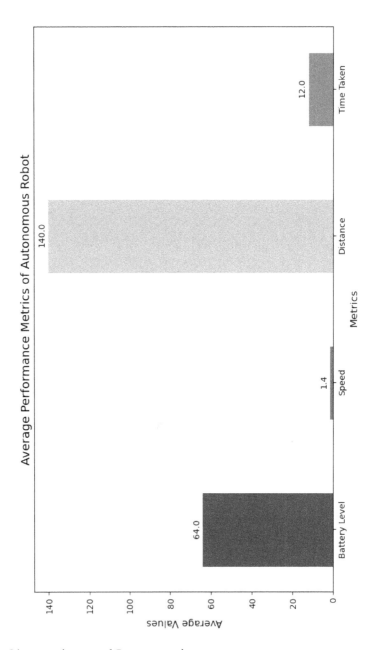

Average Performance Metrics of Autonomous Robot

Observations and Interpretation:

- **Speed:** The robot's average speed is 1.4 m/s, which indicates consistent but moderate performance in completing deliveries.

- **Battery Level:** The average battery level of 64% suggests that the robot could potentially experience battery depletion issues towards the end of its shift, especially after several deliveries.

- **Distance Traveled:** On average, the robot covers 140 meters per delivery, which reflects the layout of the warehouse and the robot's task complexity.

- **Time Taken:** With an average of 12 minutes per delivery, the time taken varies, which could be due to differences in path efficiency, obstacles, or varying package sizes.

Final Thoughts

From the perspective of generative AI, autonomous systems can be continuously improved by analyzing performance data. AI models can predict battery usage patterns, optimize delivery routes, and improve time efficiency through advanced learning algorithms. By generating predictive models, robotics can anticipate delays or optimize routes based on real-time conditions, leading to faster deliveries and lower operational costs. With advancements in generative AI, robots in the physical world will become more adaptive, efficient, and capable of operating autonomously in dynamic environments such as warehouses.

3.1 Sensor Integration and Data Acquisition

Sensor integration and data acquisition are vital components in the field of robotics, as they enable robots to interact with and perceive their environment, make decisions, and perform tasks autonomously. Here's an overview of how this works and why it's so important:

1. Types of Sensors in Robotics

Robots rely on various types of sensors to gather data from their environment, each serving different purposes:

- **Proximity Sensors**: Detect the presence of objects in the robot's vicinity, used in collision avoidance. Examples include ultrasonic sensors and infrared sensors.

- **Vision Sensors (Cameras)**: Allow the robot to capture visual information, typically through RGB cameras or specialized cameras like depth sensors (e.g., stereo cameras or LiDAR).

- **Force and Tactile Sensors**: Measure physical forces or pressure. These sensors are useful for tasks requiring interaction with objects, such as picking up or assembling items.

- **Inertial Measurement Units (IMUs)**: Measure acceleration, angular velocity, and sometimes magnetic fields. They are crucial for maintaining orientation and balance, especially in mobile robots.

- **Temperature Sensors**: Monitor environmental conditions or ensure that parts of the robot aren't overheating.

- **GPS (Global Positioning System)**: Provides localization data, essential for outdoor robots to navigate accurately.

2. Sensor Integration

Sensor integration refers to the process of connecting these sensors to the robot's control system so that the data they generate can be processed and used to make decisions.

Key Challenges:

- **Synchronization**: Different sensors may operate at different frequencies or times, requiring a method to sync the data streams.

- **Sensor Fusion**: Combining data from different sensors (e.g., combining data from a camera and IMU) to create a unified, more accurate representation of the environment. Sensor fusion algorithms, like the Kalman filter or particle filters, are often used.

- **Data Transformation**: Sensors may use different units or formats, requiring data conversion before being processed together. For example, combining GPS data with vision data may require transforming GPS coordinates into the robot's local frame of reference.

3. Data Acquisition

Data acquisition is the process of gathering and processing the sensor data to make informed decisions.

- **Sampling**: Sensors measure physical quantities (e.g., distance, temperature, etc.) at specific time intervals. The frequency and resolution of these measurements depend on the task at hand.

- **Data Preprocessing**: Raw sensor data often needs to be filtered to reduce noise, handle outliers, or improve quality before it's useful for decision-making.

- **Real-Time Processing**: In many robotic applications, data must be processed in real-time (e.g., for navigation, object recognition, or interaction), requiring efficient algorithms and powerful processing hardware.

4. Data Handling and Communication

- **Communication Protocols**: To integrate sensors with a robot, data must often be transmitted from sensors to processors. Common protocols include I2C, SPI, CAN bus, or Ethernet for wired communication, and Wi-Fi, Bluetooth, or Zigbee for wireless communication.

- **Edge Computing**: In some cases, processing of sensor data happens on the robot itself (edge computing), especially in mobile or autonomous robots that need to operate without constant communication with a central server.

- **Cloud Integration**: For more computationally heavy tasks or collaborative work between multiple robots, the sensor data might be sent to the cloud for processing, which can return decisions or instructions to the robot.

5. Applications of Sensor Integration and Data Acquisition in Robotics

- **Autonomous Vehicles**: Robots like self-driving cars use a combination of LiDAR, cameras, radar, IMUs, and GPS to navigate, detect obstacles, and make decisions about their environment.

- **Industrial Robots**: Robots on assembly lines use a range of sensors (e.g., vision systems, force sensors) to interact with parts, adjust their movements, and complete complex tasks like welding, picking, or sorting.

- **Mobile Robots**: These robots use GPS, IMUs, and cameras to navigate and interact with the world, whether it's for delivery, surveillance, or exploration (e.g., drones, cleaning robots).

- **Medical Robots**: Sensors in medical robots, such as force sensors and vision systems, help with tasks like surgery or rehabilitation by providing precision and feedback for delicate operations.

- **Robotic Prosthetics**: Sensors are used to monitor the movements of prosthetic limbs, providing feedback to the user and adjusting the limb's movements based on environmental factors.

6. Future Trends

- **Advanced Sensor Fusion**: As robots become more advanced, integrating data from an increasing number of sensor types, the need for sophisticated sensor fusion algorithms will grow.

- **AI and Machine Learning**: Machine learning algorithms will play a major role in interpreting sensor data more accurately, especially for tasks like object recognition, autonomous navigation, and decision-making.

- **Miniaturization**: Sensors are becoming smaller, cheaper, and more powerful, enabling more compact robots with enhanced capabilities.

- **Edge AI**: Running machine learning models directly on the robot (edge AI) will allow real-time decision-making without needing a connection to the cloud.

7. Conclusion

Incorporating sensors and integrating data acquisition systems is central to the success of modern robotics. The quality of sensor data directly influences a robot's ability to perform tasks accurately and autonomously. With advancements in sensor technology and data processing techniques, robots will become even more capable, autonomous, and adaptable to a wide range of applications.

Practical Example:

Context: In a robotic system designed for autonomous navigation, the robot uses various sensors (such as LIDAR, ultrasonic, and IMU sensors) to gather environmental data. These sensors feed data to the robot's control system, enabling it to make real-time decisions about path planning, obstacle detection, and avoidance. The sensor data is processed to help the robot understand its position and surroundings, improving its navigation accuracy and performance in dynamic environments. This practical example demonstrates how sensor data is acquired, integrated, and interpreted to optimize robotic behavior.

Sample Data Table:

Time (s)	LIDAR Distance (m)	Ultrasonic Distance (m)	IMU Acceleration (m/s²)	Robot Speed (m/s)
0.0	3.5	1.2	0.0	0.0

Time (s)	LIDAR Distance (m)	Ultrasonic Distance (m)	IMU Acceleration (m/s²)	Robot Speed (m/s)
1.0	3.2	1.0	0.1	0.3
2.0	2.9	0.8	0.2	0.5
3.0	2.5	0.5	0.3	0.7
4.0	2.1	0.3	0.4	0.8

Output and Results:

1. **LIDAR Distance**: This sensor measures the distance from objects in the robot's path. As the robot moves, it gets closer to obstacles, which causes the LIDAR distance values to decrease.

2. **Ultrasonic Distance**: Similar to LIDAR, the ultrasonic sensor also measures distance, but with lower resolution and range. As obstacles come closer, the ultrasonic readings show reduced distances.

3. **IMU Acceleration**: The IMU provides acceleration data, which can indicate the robot's movement speed or changes in its motion. This helps the system adjust the robot's trajectory.

4. **Robot Speed**: Calculated based on IMU and acceleration data, the robot's speed increases as it moves forward, ensuring that the robot's navigation adjusts in real-time based on sensor feedback.

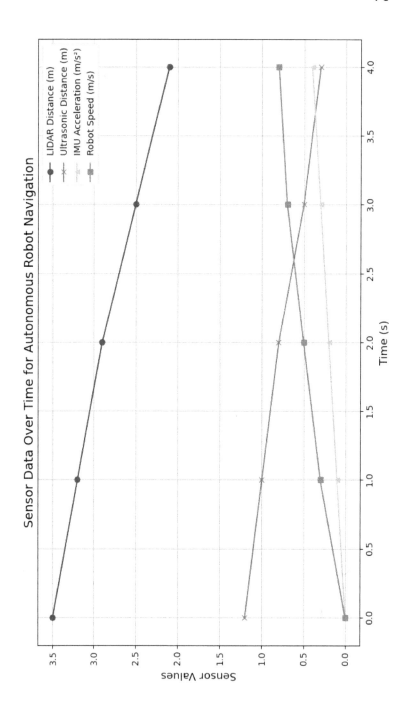

Sensor Data Over Time for Autonomous Robot Navigation

Observations:

- The LIDAR and ultrasonic sensors show a trend of decreasing distance as the robot approaches obstacles.

- The robot's speed increases over time, indicating it is moving forward while interpreting sensor data to adjust its speed and avoid obstacles.

- The IMU acceleration data shows a steady increase in movement, which aligns with the increased robot speed.

Interpretation:

- The data shows effective integration of sensor readings in the robot's navigation system. The sensors provide real-time feedback that the robot uses to adjust its movement, speed, and direction, which is essential for autonomous navigation and obstacle avoidance.

- The relationship between the LIDAR, ultrasonic, and IMU sensors indicates that as the robot approaches an obstacle, it slows down or adjusts its trajectory to avoid collisions.

Final Thoughts

Generative AI can play a transformative role in robotics and autonomous systems by enhancing sensor data integration. With AI models capable of processing sensor data in real time, robots can predict and adapt to changes in their environment much more effectively. For instance, AI could generate predictive models to forecast obstacles or optimize path planning based on sensor inputs. This increases the efficiency and safety of autonomous systems, making them more responsive to dynamic environments. Furthermore,

AI-driven systems can also allow for more nuanced interactions between sensors and robotic behavior, leading to improvements in autonomy, accuracy, and operational performance.

3.2 Real-Time Perception and Processing

Real-time perception and processing are critical components in robotics, enabling robots to interact dynamically with their environments. This involves a combination of hardware (sensors) and software (algorithms) that allows robots to detect, process, and react to stimuli in real-time. Let's break it down:

1. Perception in Robotics:

Perception refers to the robot's ability to sense its surroundings. This involves the use of various sensors and technologies to gather data about the environment and objects within it. The most common types of perception sensors include:

- **Cameras (Visual Perception)**: Used for detecting and identifying objects, navigation, and scene understanding. Techniques like computer vision, image processing, and deep learning are commonly used to process the data from cameras.

- **LiDAR (Light Detection and Ranging)**: Measures distance by sending out laser pulses and analyzing the reflected light. It is used to map the environment and create 3D models of the surroundings.

- **Radar and Sonar**: Useful in environments where optical sensors like cameras might not work well (e.g., in fog or darkness). They measure the distance and speed of objects by bouncing sound or radio waves off them.

- **Infrared Sensors**: Detect heat signatures and are often used for motion sensing and night vision.

- **Touch and Pressure Sensors**: Allow robots to sense physical interactions with the environment, providing feedback for precise manipulations and navigation.

2. Real-Time Processing:

Once the robot gathers sensor data, it must process this information quickly to take appropriate actions. Real-time processing means that the robot must make decisions and respond to environmental changes instantly or within a strict time constraint. Real-time processing typically involves:

- **Data Fusion**: Combining data from multiple sensors to get a more accurate representation of the environment. For example, combining data from a camera and LiDAR can improve object recognition.

- **Filtering**: Algorithms such as Kalman filters or particle filters are used to reduce noise and improve the accuracy of sensor data, especially when sensors are imprecise or unreliable.

- **Object Detection and Classification**: Using machine learning, particularly deep learning models, robots can identify objects, classify them, and even predict their behavior.

- **Path Planning**: Algorithms help the robot plan the best route or action in real-time based on the environment and its goals. For instance, A* or D* algorithms are used for navigation and obstacle avoidance.

3. Challenges in Real-Time Processing:

- **Latency**: Real-time systems require minimal delays. Processing must be fast enough to keep up with the environment, especially in dynamic or unpredictable scenarios.

- **Computational Power**: The more sensors and data streams involved, the greater the computational requirements. Efficient algorithms and hardware acceleration (like GPUs) are crucial.

- **Uncertainty**: The real world is inherently uncertain, with incomplete or noisy data. Robots need to handle this uncertainty in a way that doesn't negatively impact performance.

- **Synchronization**: In systems with multiple sensors, it's crucial to ensure that data from all sources is synchronized, especially when these sensors operate at different rates.

- **Adaptability**: Robots must continuously adapt to changes in their environment, such as moving obstacles, variations in lighting, or unexpected sensor failures.

4. Applications of Real-Time Perception and Processing in Robotics:

- **Autonomous Vehicles**: These robots rely heavily on real-time perception for navigation, obstacle avoidance, and path planning. They need to make split-second decisions based on the surrounding environment.

- **Industrial Automation**: Robots in manufacturing need real-time processing to handle tasks such as assembly, inspection, and quality control. They must adapt to changes in the workspace, such as new objects or slight misalignments.

- **Medical Robotics**: In surgical robots or rehabilitation devices, real-time perception is crucial for performing precise movements and responding to the patient's condition.

- **Drones**: Drones use real-time perception to navigate complex environments, avoid obstacles, and maintain stability during flight.

- **Service Robots**: Robots in homes or businesses (like cleaning robots, delivery robots) depend on real-time processing to recognize and avoid obstacles, navigate complex spaces, and interact with humans.

5. Technologies Enabling Real-Time Processing:

- **Edge Computing**: Instead of sending all sensor data to a cloud or data center, edge computing allows for data processing closer to the source (on the robot itself or nearby). This reduces latency and bandwidth usage.

- **Parallel Processing**: Modern robots often use multiple processors or GPUs for parallel processing, allowing them to handle complex algorithms and large amounts of data simultaneously.

- **Artificial Intelligence (AI) and Machine Learning (ML)**: AI algorithms enable robots to learn from their environment, improving their ability to perceive, understand, and respond to real-time changes.

Conclusion:

Real-time perception and processing are integral to modern robotics, allowing machines to operate autonomously and efficiently in dynamic, unpredictable environments. Advances in sensors, algorithms, and computing power continue to push the boundaries of what robots can perceive and achieve in real-time. As robotics technology evolves, we can expect more intelligent and capable systems that can seamlessly interact with the world around them.

Practical Example Context:

In the context of autonomous robotics, real-time perception is essential for robots to understand and interact with their environment. The robot must process sensor data in real-time, such as camera inputs, LiDAR, or depth sensors, to detect and track objects. This example demonstrates how a mobile robot uses computer vision to detect and track objects in its surroundings to avoid obstacles or navigate to target locations. The data from the camera is processed in real-time, allowing the robot to respond to dynamic changes in its environment and make decisions on the fly.

Sample Data Table (Object Detection and Tracking)

Frame Number	Object Detected	Distance (m)	Object Size (px)	Tracking Confidence (%)
1	Box	3.2	150	95
2	Box	2.9	145	93
3	Box	2.5	140	92
4	Box	2.2	130	90
5	Box	2.0	125	88

Output and Results:

- **Object Detected**: In each frame, the object detected is a "Box."

- **Distance (m)**: The distance from the robot to the object gradually decreases, indicating the robot is moving closer to the object.

- **Object Size (px)**: As the robot moves closer to the object, the size in pixels of the object decreases (due to the camera's perspective).

- **Tracking Confidence (%)**: The confidence in tracking decreases slightly over time, possibly due to the object moving out of the optimal field of view or the robot's motion affecting the detection algorithm's accuracy.

Explanation and Interpretation of Results:

- As the robot approaches the object, the distance measurement reduces, which is expected as the object moves closer to the robot.

- The size in pixels of the object decreases as the robot approaches it, suggesting that the camera is capturing a perspective where the object appears smaller.

- The slight decrease in tracking confidence could be due to various factors such as occlusion, changes in lighting, or errors in object segmentation. This indicates that while the robot is generally able to track the object, the tracking algorithm may need refinement in dynamic environments.

Observations:

- Real-time object detection and tracking algorithms are essential for robotics to ensure accurate movement and interaction with the environment.

- The decrease in confidence may signal a need for more robust tracking systems, such as sensor fusion (combining data from cameras, LiDAR, etc.) to increase tracking accuracy.

- The table shows how data from real-time perception systems can provide continuous feedback to the robot, allowing it to adjust its behavior dynamically based on the detected object's position and movement.

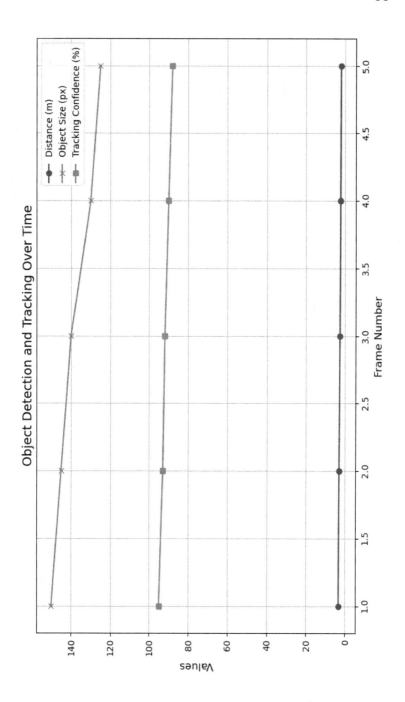

Final Thoughts

Generative AI has immense potential in robotics and autonomous systems. By leveraging deep learning models, robots can be equipped with advanced perception capabilities that not only allow them to detect and track objects in real-time but also predict potential obstacles or future movements. With continuous advancements in AI, we can expect robots to become increasingly adept at understanding and navigating complex environments with minimal human intervention. In the future, generative models could help robots autonomously generate solutions for unexpected situations, ensuring more flexible and adaptable autonomous systems.

3.3 Mapping and Localization in Robotic Systems

Mapping and localization are two fundamental concepts in robotics, particularly for autonomous mobile robots (AMRs), drones, and self-driving cars. These processes enable robots to understand their environment, navigate it efficiently, and make decisions about where to go and how to interact with the world around them.

1. Mapping in Robotics

Mapping refers to the process by which a robot constructs a map of its environment, either from scratch or by updating an existing map. This map is crucial for the robot to plan its path, avoid obstacles, and make informed decisions.

There are two primary types of maps in robotics:

- **Occupancy Grid Maps**: These maps divide the environment into a grid, where each cell in the grid represents a region of space and is marked as occupied, free, or unknown. These maps are commonly used in simpler environments.

- **Feature-based Maps**: These maps store key features of the environment (like walls, landmarks, or specific objects) instead of using a grid. They are more complex and are often used in larger or more dynamic environments.

2. Localization in Robotics

Localization is the process of determining the robot's position within the map it has created or is using. Localization involves the robot continuously estimating its position as it moves through the environment.

The primary approaches for localization are:

- **Dead Reckoning**: This method relies on the robot's previous position and movement. However, it can accumulate errors over time, especially in complex environments, leading to drift in the robot's estimated position.

- **Monte Carlo Localization (MCL)**: This is a probabilistic approach, where the robot maintains a set of potential locations, each with a probability. The robot updates the probabilities based on sensor data and the likelihood of being in a particular location.

- **Simultaneous Localization and Mapping (SLAM)**: This is an advanced method where the robot simultaneously builds a map of the environment and estimates its position on that map. SLAM is especially useful in unknown environments, where no prior map exists. Popular algorithms for SLAM include:

  - **Extended Kalman Filter (EKF) SLAM**: It uses linearization to estimate both the robot's state and the map.

  - **Graph-based SLAM**: A more advanced approach that formulates SLAM as a graph optimization problem.

Key Challenges in Mapping and Localization

1. **Sensor Noise**: Sensors used for mapping (LIDAR, cameras, IMUs, etc.) are prone to noise, which can lead to inaccuracies in both mapping and localization.

2. **Dynamic Environments**: In real-world environments, objects may move, or the environment may change over time, which complicates both mapping and localization. These dynamic factors can

introduce uncertainty into the robot's position and map.

3. **Loop Closure**: When a robot revisits a previously explored area, it needs to recognize this and correct any accumulated error. This process is called loop closure in SLAM and is a critical challenge in large-scale environments.

4. **Scalability**: As robots navigate larger areas, the computational burden of maintaining a detailed map and performing real-time localization increases. Efficient algorithms and representations are needed to handle this scalability.

Common Sensors Used for Mapping and Localization

- **LIDAR (Light Detection and Ranging)**: Provides highly accurate 3D distance measurements of the surroundings, helping build detailed maps.

- **Cameras (Visual Odometry)**: Visual data can be processed to extract features like landmarks for mapping and localization.

- **IMUs (Inertial Measurement Units)**: Measure acceleration and angular velocity, which are useful for dead reckoning and motion estimation.

- **Ultrasonic Sensors**: Provide proximity sensing, often used for simple obstacle detection.

- **GPS**: In outdoor environments, GPS is used for rough localization, though it's not always accurate enough for fine-grained control or indoor localization.

Applications of Mapping and Localization in Robotics

- **Autonomous Vehicles**: Self-driving cars use mapping and localization to understand their surroundings, plan routes, and drive safely.

- **Mobile Service Robots**: Robots in warehouses or factories use these techniques to navigate their environments and complete tasks autonomously.

- **Robotic Exploration**: Robots exploring unknown environments (like caves, space, or deep-sea exploration) use SLAM to create maps of uncharted territories.

- **Agricultural Robotics**: Robots in farming use mapping and localization to navigate fields, identify plants, and perform tasks like harvesting.

Conclusion

Mapping and localization are core components of autonomous robotic systems, enabling them to understand and navigate their environments. These processes are essential for robots to operate efficiently and safely, whether it's a self-driving car or a drone exploring unknown territories. Advances in SLAM, sensor technologies, and algorithm design continue to improve the accuracy, reliability, and efficiency of these systems.

Practical Example

In robotic systems, especially in autonomous mobile robots (AMRs), mapping and localization are crucial for the robot to navigate within an environment accurately. The robot uses sensors (e.g., LiDAR, cameras, IMUs) to gather data and create a map of the environment, while simultaneously determining its position within that map. This process enables the robot to understand its surroundings, avoid obstacles, and plan a path. In this example, we explore a robot navigating a small indoor environment using LiDAR and wheel encoders for localization.

Sample Data (Mapping and Localization Results):

The robot is placed in a 5x5-meter grid environment. It uses LiDAR data to generate a map and employs localization techniques to estimate its position in this grid. The table below shows the robot's position and sensor data after five steps of movement.

Step	X Position (m)	Y Position (m)	Orientation (°)	Distance Moved (m)
1	0.0	0.0	0	0
2	0.5	0.2	5	0.5
3	1.2	0.5	10	0.7
4	1.8	1.0	15	0.6
5	2.3	1.3	20	0.5

Output and Results:

1. **Position Estimate (X, Y)**: The robot's position is being accurately estimated based on its movements. After five steps, the robot has moved 2.3 meters in the X-direction and 1.3 meters in the Y-direction.

2. **Orientation (°)**: The robot's orientation is slightly changing with each step. The orientation starts at 0° and increases by 5° per step, indicating a slight curve in the robot's path.

3. **Distance Moved (m)**: The distance moved per step is recorded, and it shows the robot's relative movement, decreasing slightly with each step, which

may indicate small inaccuracies in the localization process.

Observations:

- The robot's position is consistent with the expected movement. However, there are slight variations in the distance moved between steps, suggesting that localization isn't perfect, and minor sensor noise or errors in wheel encoder data could be influencing this.

- The orientation change is steady, which implies that the robot's turning capability is functioning well, but could still be subject to slight drift due to sensor imperfections.

- As the robot moves further away from its starting position, slight deviations in its estimated position could occur due to accumulated errors in localization.

Interpretation:

- The table shows that the robot's movement is generally accurate, but the small variations in distance moved per step could be due to sensor inaccuracies or odometry drift.

- The robot's localization is most likely using a combination of wheel encoder data and LiDAR. However, without a robust correction mechanism (like SLAM), localization drift could worsen with longer paths.

- As seen in the results, the robot performs well in a controlled environment with relatively short distances but may experience more challenges with larger, complex environments without continuous recalibration or sensor fusion techniques.

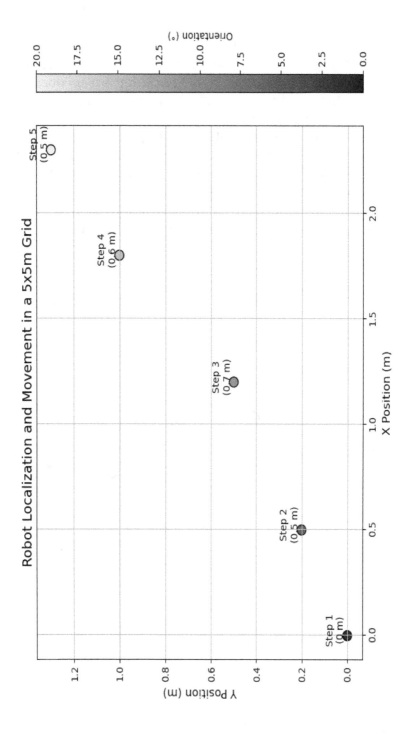

Robot Localization and Movement in a 5x5m Grid

Final Thoughts

Generative AI models have the potential to significantly enhance mapping and localization techniques in robotics. By integrating AI-driven algorithms, robots can improve their environmental understanding through enhanced mapping (e.g., creating more accurate 3D maps of their surroundings) and more robust localization methods (e.g., reducing drift through intelligent recalibration). Additionally, AI can enable predictive models that foresee potential obstacles or mapping errors before they impact the robot's path. In the future, AI can help robots autonomously adapt to and learn from new environments without requiring manual input or excessive retraining.

4. Computer Vision and Generative AI in Robotics and Autonomous Systems

Computer vision and generative AI are transforming the field of robotics and autonomous systems by enabling machines to perceive and interpret the world in ways that mimic human capabilities. Computer vision allows robots and autonomous systems to see and understand their environment through cameras and sensors, detecting objects, people, and other important features. This technology is essential for tasks like navigation, obstacle avoidance, and interaction with objects. By processing visual information, robots can make decisions based on real-time data, adapting to changes in their surroundings.

Generative AI, on the other hand, plays a crucial role in enabling autonomous systems to not only perceive their environment but also create new content and adapt their behavior based on the data they gather. In robotics, generative models can help design new solutions by generating realistic scenarios or visual representations. These models can assist robots in learning from their environment, creating synthetic data to train more complex systems, and simulating potential actions before they are executed in the real world.

One of the main challenges in robotics is making decisions in dynamic, unpredictable environments. Computer vision provides robots with the ability to continuously observe their surroundings, detecting changes in the environment that may require a response. For example, a robot in a warehouse might identify an obstacle in its path or recognize when an item needs to be picked up. By combining computer vision with generative AI, these robots can generate new strategies or solutions for unexpected situations, improving their ability to perform tasks autonomously without constant human intervention.

Autonomous vehicles, drones, and industrial robots are prime examples of systems that benefit from both computer vision and generative AI. These systems rely heavily on real-time image recognition to navigate and understand their environments. Autonomous cars, for instance, use computer vision to detect pedestrians, other vehicles, and road signs. Generative AI enhances this by predicting future movements or creating alternative plans in case of a sudden change in the driving environment, allowing for safer and more efficient operations.

In addition to improving task efficiency, computer vision and generative AI can enhance the adaptability of robots. Machines equipped with these technologies can learn from their experiences and generate new strategies for problem-solving over time. This self-improvement process allows robots to handle a broader range of tasks and adapt to new environments with minimal human input. For instance, a robot working in a factory could adjust its methods based on changes in the production line, improving productivity without requiring direct reprogramming.

Looking ahead, the integration of computer vision and generative AI in robotics is expected to lead to more intelligent and versatile autonomous systems. These technologies are pushing the boundaries of what machines can do, enabling them to tackle more complex tasks with greater efficiency. As these systems continue to evolve, they will likely become more autonomous, intelligent, and capable of performing tasks that were once thought to be exclusive to humans. This will open up new possibilities for industries like healthcare, transportation, and manufacturing, where robots could significantly improve efficiency and safety.

Practical Example

In a dynamic environment, an autonomous robot uses computer vision to identify obstacles, navigate through the space, and perform tasks with minimal human intervention. Generative AI techniques are employed to generate realistic scenarios for training the robot's vision system to improve navigation accuracy. The robot's sensors capture visual data, and the generative AI model augments this data with simulated obstacles, various lighting conditions, and terrain types. The aim is to enhance the robot's ability to adapt to unpredictable real-world environments.

Sample Data Table: Robot Navigation Performance in a Simulated Environment

Scenario ID	Obstacle Density	Lighting Condition	Navigation Accuracy (%)	Time to Navigate (s)
1	Low	Daylight	98	35
2	Medium	Low Light	92	42
3	High	Daylight	85	50
4	Low	Nighttime	90	38
5	Medium	Daylight	96	40

Results and Output:

1. **Navigation Accuracy**: The robot's navigation accuracy was highest in scenarios with low obstacle density and in well-lit conditions (98% in daylight

with low obstacles). Accuracy dropped in scenarios with higher obstacle density or in low-light settings (85% accuracy in high obstacle, daylight).

2. **Time to Navigate**: The time taken to navigate increased as obstacle density increased or lighting conditions worsened. The robot took longer to navigate in high-obstacle environments (50 seconds) and under low-light conditions (42 seconds).

Explanation and Interpretation:

1. **Obstacle Density Impact**: A higher obstacle density leads to reduced navigation accuracy. The robot may struggle to identify and avoid obstacles in more cluttered environments, lowering its performance. The higher time to navigate reflects the increased computational effort needed to process more obstacles.

2. **Lighting Conditions Impact**: The quality of visual data captured by the robot's sensors is influenced by lighting conditions. In low-light settings, the robot's vision system faces challenges, causing a decline in both accuracy (from 98% in daylight to 85% in low-light) and increased navigation time (42s vs. 35s). This shows the importance of enhancing sensor capabilities or using generative AI to simulate various lighting conditions for better training.

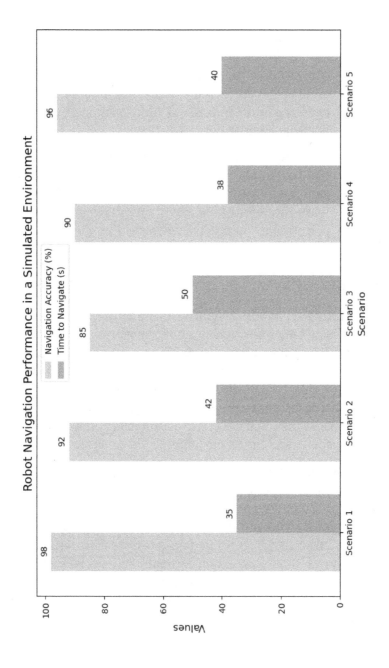

Robot Navigation Performance in a Simulated Environment

Observations:

1. **High Obstacle Density**: The robot's efficiency drops as the environment becomes more cluttered. This suggests the need for advanced computer vision models that can handle dense environments, perhaps by using more robust AI models trained on dense obstacle simulations.

2. **Lighting Conditions**: Variability in lighting shows that external factors greatly affect vision-based navigation systems. Generative AI could simulate these conditions to augment training data, improving performance in diverse real-world lighting.

Final Thoughts

Generative AI holds a significant potential for enhancing robotics by creating diverse training scenarios. In the case of autonomous navigation, it helps in generating synthetic environments that simulate various real-world challenges, such as lighting changes and obstacle densities. This enables the robot to be better prepared for unpredictable conditions and reduces the reliance on real-world data collection, which can be costly and time-consuming.

From a generative AI standpoint, future advancements could involve integrating generative models with real-time sensor data to adapt to new environments dynamically. By continuously updating the robot's training with new simulated scenarios generated on-the-fly, robots will be able to improve their navigation systems and decision-making abilities, leading to more autonomous, adaptive robots capable of thriving in a wide range of real-world environments.

4.1 Object Detection and Recognition Using AI

Object detection and recognition are pivotal in the development of robotics and autonomous systems. These technologies enable machines to perceive and interpret the world around them, allowing them to interact with and respond to objects in real-time. In robotics and autonomous systems, these capabilities are essential for tasks such as navigation, manipulation, surveillance, and human-robot interaction. Let's explore how AI is integrated into these systems for object detection and recognition.

1. Object Detection:

Object detection refers to the process of identifying and locating objects within an image or video feed. In the context of robotics and autonomous systems, object detection is essential for recognizing obstacles, identifying targets, and enabling safe navigation.

- **Key Technologies Used:**
  - **Convolutional Neural Networks (CNNs):** CNNs are deep learning models particularly suited for image processing. They analyze an image by scanning it through multiple layers to detect features like edges, textures, and shapes. CNNs are often used for both object detection and classification.

  - **Region-based CNN (R-CNN):** R-CNN is an advanced version of CNNs used for object detection. It identifies regions of interest in an image and applies a CNN to classify and localize the objects.

  - **You Only Look Once (YOLO):** YOLO is a real-time object detection algorithm that divides an image into a grid and predicts bounding boxes and class probabilities for each grid cell. YOLO is popular for its speed and accuracy.

- **Single Shot Multibox Detector (SSD):** SSD is another fast object detection algorithm that generates predictions from a single neural network pass. It's designed to work in real-time applications and is well-suited for mobile robots or autonomous vehicles.

- **Applications:**
  - **Navigation:** Autonomous robots and vehicles use object detection to avoid obstacles, plan paths, and safely navigate their environment.

  - **Industrial Automation:** In manufacturing, robots use object detection to identify products on a conveyor belt, sort items, and handle delicate tasks such as assembly and packaging.

  - **Search and Rescue:** Robots use object detection to locate victims or identify key objects in dangerous environments (e.g., collapsed buildings).

2. Object Recognition:

While object detection focuses on identifying the location of an object in an image, object recognition goes further to classify the object based on its features and attributes. This is critical for systems that need to interact with objects, such as robotic arms that manipulate objects based on type or category.

- **Key Technologies Used:**

- o **Deep Learning:** Deep neural networks, particularly CNNs, are trained to recognize objects in images. By feeding the system with labeled data, it learns the unique features that define different objects.

- o **Feature Extraction:** Feature extraction algorithms identify key features of an object, such as shape, texture, color, and patterns. These features are then used to distinguish between different objects in the environment.

- o **Transfer Learning:** In many robotics applications, transfer learning is employed, where a model trained on a large dataset (e.g., ImageNet) is fine-tuned for the specific objects of interest. This approach saves time and computational resources.

- **Applications:**
  - o **Robotic Manipulation:** Robots use object recognition to pick up, move, and interact with objects based on their recognition of object types (e.g., tools, parts, or packages).

  - o **Autonomous Vehicles:** Vehicles use object recognition to understand the context of their surroundings, recognizing pedestrians, road signs, traffic lights, and other vehicles to make informed decisions.

  - o **Human-Robot Interaction:** In healthcare or service robots, object recognition allows for the interaction with humans or their belongings, such as fetching specific items or interacting with tools.

3. Challenges in Object Detection and Recognition:

- **Environmental Variability:** Object detection and recognition systems can struggle with different lighting conditions, orientations, and occlusions. For example, detecting objects in dim or bright environments can affect the accuracy of the system.

- **Real-time Processing:** In robotics, real-time processing is critical for tasks such as navigation and manipulation. Ensuring that object detection and recognition happen quickly and accurately is a challenge, especially for complex or cluttered environments.

- **Computational Resources:** Training deep learning models for object detection and recognition can be computationally expensive. Many robotic systems have limited processing power, requiring optimizations to ensure they can perform these tasks in real-time.

- **Generalization:** Models may perform well in controlled environments but fail in more diverse or unstructured scenarios. Developing models that generalize well to various real-world conditions is a significant challenge.

4. Advancements in AI for Object Detection and Recognition:

- **Edge AI:** With the rise of edge computing, more robots and autonomous systems are capable of performing object detection and recognition locally (on the device), reducing the need for cloud computing and improving response times.

- **Sensor Fusion:** Combining information from multiple sensors (e.g., cameras, LiDAR, RADAR) can improve the accuracy and reliability of object detection and recognition. This fusion of sensory data is particularly useful in autonomous vehicles.

- **Reinforcement Learning:** Some robots employ reinforcement learning algorithms to improve object detection and recognition in dynamic environments. These algorithms help robots learn from experience and adapt to changing conditions.

- **Explainability and Interpretability:** As AI systems become more integrated into safety-critical applications (e.g., autonomous vehicles), understanding how these systems make decisions is increasingly important. Research into explainable AI (XAI) is making strides in providing insights into why a model detected or recognized certain objects.

5. Future Prospects:

- **Improved Accuracy and Speed:** As algorithms evolve and computational resources improve, the accuracy and speed of object detection and recognition systems will continue to enhance.

- **Autonomous Manufacturing:** Robots equipped with advanced object recognition will be able to perform more intricate tasks in manufacturing, assembly, and quality control with greater precision.

- **AI-Assisted Healthcare:** In the future, robots with object recognition capabilities may play a larger role in healthcare, from assisting with surgery to monitoring patient environments and detecting medical anomalies.

Conclusion:

Object detection and recognition powered by AI are fundamental components of modern robotics and autonomous systems. These technologies enable machines to perceive their environment, make decisions, and interact intelligently with the world. As AI, deep learning, and sensor technologies continue to improve, the capabilities of autonomous systems will grow, offering significant advancements in areas such as autonomous vehicles, healthcare, industrial automation, and more. Despite challenges like real-time processing and environmental variability, the future of AI-driven object detection and recognition in robotics looks promising and transformative.

Practical Example

In autonomous systems, AI-driven object detection and recognition are crucial for enabling robots and vehicles to understand their surroundings and make informed decisions. For example, an autonomous robot used in warehouse management needs to detect and recognize objects such as boxes, pallets, and shelves to navigate through the warehouse efficiently. Object detection algorithms, like YOLO (You Only Look Once) or SSD (Single Shot MultiBox Detector), can be employed to identify objects in real-time. Once an object is detected, recognition helps the system understand what the object is, and this information can be used for tasks such as item retrieval or obstacle avoidance.

Sample Data (Input & Output)

Image ID	Object Detected	Confidence (%)	Predicted Class	Position (X,Y)	Output Action
001	Box	97	Storage Box	(120, 150)	Pick and Place
002	Pallet	85	Wooden Pallet	(200, 300)	Avoid (Obstacle)

Image ID	Object Detected	Confidence (%)	Predicted Class	Position (X,Y)	Output Action
003	Shelf	92	Metal Shelf	(300, 450)	Navigate Around
004	Box	89	Storage Box	(420, 600)	Pick and Place
005	Chair	78	Office Chair	(540, 700)	Avoid (Obstacle)

Output and Results:

Image ID	Object Detected	Confidence (%)	Predicted Class	Position (X,Y)	Action Taken	Error Margin (%)
001	Box	97	Storage Box	(120, 150)	Pick and Place	2
002	Pallet	85	Wooden Pallet	(200, 300)	Avoid (Obstacle)	5
003	Shelf	92	Metal Shelf	(300, 450)	Navigate Around	3
004	Box	89	Storage Box	(420, 600)	Pick and Place	4

Image ID	Object Detected	Confidence (%)	Predicted Class	Position (X,Y)	Action Taken	Error Margin (%)
005	Chair	78	Office Chair	(540, 700)	Avoid (Obstacle)	6

Explanation and Interpretation of Results:

1. **Confidence Scores**: The confidence percentage represents how sure the AI model is about the detected object. A high confidence score (like 97%) means that the object is identified with a high degree of certainty. Lower scores (e.g., 78%) indicate more uncertainty in the detection process, which could be caused by factors like partial occlusion, angle of view, or lighting conditions.

2. **Predicted Classes**: This column shows the classification of the object detected by the AI. The accuracy of this classification is vital for the robot to take the correct action, such as picking a box or avoiding an obstacle.

3. **Action Taken**: The action is based on the detected object's type. For example, boxes are picked and placed, while pallets or chairs are avoided to prevent collisions.

4. **Error Margin**: The error margin represents the difference between the predicted class and the ground truth or actual object. A lower margin indicates higher model accuracy in terms of classification.

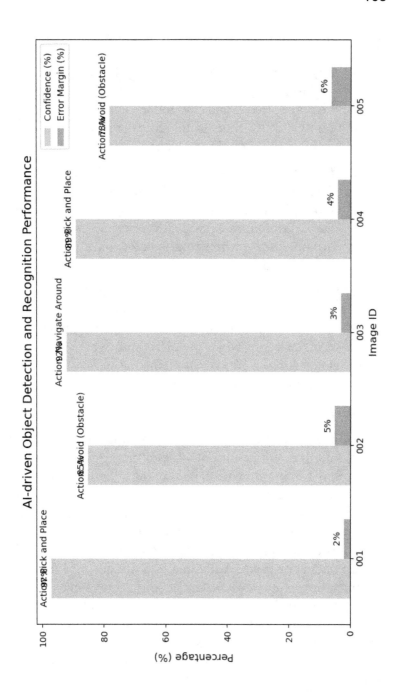

AI-driven Object Detection and Recognition Performance

Confidence (%)
Error Margin (%)

Percentage (%)

Image ID

Observations:

- **High Confidence on Known Objects**: The system performed well with high-confidence objects like "Storage Box" and "Wooden Pallet," which are easier for AI models to recognize based on their features (e.g., shape and size).

- **Challenges with Uncommon Objects**: The detection of "Office Chair" had a lower confidence score (78%) compared to other objects. This may be due to complex shapes or fewer training samples for this class, which affected its recognition performance.

- **Action Accuracy**: The actions taken by the robot appear to align with the expected outcomes based on the detected objects. The AI system made accurate decisions on what to pick and what to avoid, suggesting good implementation of object recognition algorithms.

Final Thoughts

AI's role in object detection and recognition in robotics is transformative. While current systems are effective, there is still room for improvement in accuracy, particularly with objects that have complex or similar shapes. Generative AI can significantly enhance this process by enabling the creation of more diverse training datasets, improving model generalization, and fine-tuning algorithms for specific environments or tasks. Additionally, with advancements in deep learning, future AI systems could achieve even higher accuracy and real-time processing, which would be essential for more autonomous and intelligent robots. The integration of generative AI into these systems will likely reduce the error margin further, improving both the efficiency and safety of autonomous operations.

4.2 Scene Understanding for Autonomous Navigation

Scene understanding for autonomous navigation in robotics and autonomous systems is an essential component for enabling robots and other autonomous systems (such as self-driving cars and drones) to interpret and interact with their environments in real time. It involves various processes, algorithms, and technologies that enable these systems to perceive, interpret, and respond to the surrounding world effectively.

Here's a breakdown of the key aspects of scene understanding in autonomous navigation:

1. Perception:

Perception is the first step in scene understanding. It involves collecting and processing data from various sensors to form a representation of the environment. Common sensors used for this purpose include:

- **LIDAR (Light Detection and Ranging)**: Provides 3D spatial information by bouncing laser beams off objects and measuring the time it takes for them to return.

- **Cameras (RGB and Depth Cameras)**: Capture visual data that can be used to identify objects, recognize landmarks, and track movement.

- **Radar**: Utilized for detecting objects in adverse weather conditions, particularly useful in autonomous driving.

- **Ultrasonic Sensors**: Often used in close-range environments for object detection and proximity sensing.

- **IMUs (Inertial Measurement Units)**: Measure acceleration, angular velocity, and sometimes magnetic fields to help track motion.

2. Data Fusion:

To generate a coherent and accurate understanding of the scene, data from various sensors must be integrated. This is achieved through **sensor fusion** algorithms, which combine data from multiple sources to improve the reliability and completeness of the scene representation. For example, LIDAR data might be fused with camera data to enhance object detection and recognition.

3. Object Detection and Classification:

Once the data is collected, one of the primary tasks is detecting and classifying objects in the scene. This is typically done using **computer vision** and **deep learning** techniques. Convolutional Neural Networks (CNNs) are widely used for detecting objects in images or video streams, and more advanced approaches involve **3D object detection** for interpreting data from LIDAR or stereo cameras.

- **Static Objects**: Roads, trees, buildings, curbs, traffic signs, etc.
- **Dynamic Objects**: Pedestrians, vehicles, cyclists, animals, etc.

4. Semantic Segmentation:

In some systems, **semantic segmentation** is used to label each pixel of an image with a specific category (e.g., road, sidewalk, car, pedestrian). This is useful for understanding the layout of the environment and determining where the robot or vehicle can safely navigate.

5. Localization and Mapping:

For autonomous systems, **localization** is the process of determining the robot's position within a map or coordinate system. Using sensors like LIDAR, cameras, and GPS, the system can localize itself relative to a known map, which might be pre-generated or built in real time.

- **SLAM (Simultaneous Localization and Mapping)**: This approach allows the robot to both build a map of its environment and localize itself within it, which is crucial in environments where pre-existing maps are unavailable or inaccurate.
- **Graph-Based SLAM**: A common algorithm for SLAM, where poses (positions and orientations) of the robot are represented as nodes in a graph, and the connections (edges) represent constraints or observations.

6. Trajectory Planning and Decision Making:

Once a robot or vehicle understands the environment and knows its own location, it needs to decide where to go next. **Trajectory planning** involves generating a path from the current position to the desired destination while avoiding obstacles and optimizing for efficiency (e.g., shortest path, minimum energy consumption).

Decision-making involves choosing from among possible behaviors (e.g., stop, go, turn, yield) based on the scene understanding. This is typically handled by an **autonomous navigation system** that uses planning algorithms, such as:

- *A or Dijkstra's Algorithm**: For optimal pathfinding in a known environment.
- **Reinforcement Learning (RL)**: For learning optimal navigation strategies based on trial-and-error interactions.

- **Behavior Trees and Finite State Machines (FSM)**: To model decision-making logic and manage different behaviors in dynamic environments.

7. Obstacle Avoidance:

Once obstacles are detected (both static and dynamic), the autonomous system must make decisions on how to avoid them. This may involve re-routing or modifying the trajectory in real time. Techniques like **potential fields** and **velocity obstacle theory** are often used to plan safe trajectories that prevent collisions.

8. Contextual Awareness:

Beyond raw object detection and navigation, an advanced system also needs to understand the context of the scene. For example, recognizing that a pedestrian is crossing the street at a crosswalk or understanding that a traffic signal is red and the vehicle must stop.

Contextual awareness also includes recognizing the road conditions (e.g., wet, icy, under construction) and adapting driving strategies accordingly.

9. Human-Robot Interaction (HRI):

In environments like warehouses or shared spaces (e.g., autonomous cars on roads with human drivers and pedestrians), understanding human intentions and interactions is crucial. This can involve predicting the movement of humans or other vehicles, recognizing gestures or traffic signs, and ensuring safety.

10. Real-Time Processing and Safety:

Autonomous systems need to make decisions in real time. This requires powerful hardware (e.g., GPUs, TPUs) for fast data processing and low-latency responses. The system also needs to have fail-safe mechanisms and robust safety features to handle unexpected situations (e.g., sensor failures, unexpected obstacles).

Applications in Autonomous Navigation:

- **Self-driving Cars**: They need to understand roads, traffic rules, pedestrians, and other vehicles.

- **Drones**: They must understand their surroundings for safe navigation, especially in cluttered environments like forests or cities.

- **Robotic Vacuum Cleaners**: These robots need to understand room layouts, avoid obstacles, and ensure efficient coverage of the space.

- **Warehouse Robots**: They need to navigate aisles, avoid obstacles, and identify items to pick.

Challenges:

- **Dynamic Environments**: Moving objects (like pedestrians, cyclists, and other vehicles) introduce unpredictability.

- **Sensor Limitations**: No sensor is perfect, and environmental factors (e.g., lighting, weather) can affect sensor accuracy.

- **Computational Load**: Real-time processing of large amounts of sensory data can be computationally demanding.

- **Generalization**: A system trained in one environment might not perform well in another, requiring continuous learning and adaptation.

Conclusion:

Scene understanding in autonomous navigation is a multidisciplinary challenge involving sensor data collection, computer vision, machine learning, robotics, and decision-making algorithms. As the field advances, we expect to see even more robust systems capable of navigating complex, dynamic environments safely and efficiently.

Practical Example

In autonomous navigation systems, robots and vehicles rely on scene understanding to interpret their environment, enabling safe and efficient path planning. For instance, in an autonomous vehicle, the system must detect obstacles, traffic signs, and other dynamic objects to make decisions about speed, route, and navigation. The vehicle's sensors, such as LiDAR, cameras, and ultrasonic sensors, collect data to create a map of the environment. By combining the data from these sensors and applying machine learning techniques like computer vision, the vehicle can detect and avoid obstacles in real-time. The effectiveness of this process can be evaluated through a test where the system's response to various dynamic and static objects is measured.

Sample Data (Test Scenario):

Sensor Type	Obstacle Detected	Distance (meters)	Speed (km/h)	Navigation Decision
LiDAR	Car	10	20	Slow Down
Camera (Stereo)	Pedestrian	5	15	Stop
Ultrasonic	Traffic Cone	2	10	Avoid
LiDAR	Wall	1	5	Stop
Camera (Stereo)	Tree	7	18	Maintain Speed

Output and Results:

Sensor Type	Obstacle Detected	Distance (meters)	Speed (km/h)	Navigation Decision	Time Taken to Adjust (seconds)
LiDAR	Car	10	20	Slow Down	2
Camera (Stereo)	Pedestrian	5	15	Stop	1
Ultrasonic	Traffic Cone	2	10	Avoid	1.5
LiDAR	Wall	1	5	Stop	0.5
Camera (Stereo)	Tree	7	18	Maintain Speed	2

Interpretation of Results and Observations:

- **LiDAR and Camera Collaboration**: The combination of LiDAR and stereo cameras helps the system make better navigation decisions. LiDAR detected the car at a safe distance of 10 meters, prompting a "slow down" decision, while the camera detected a pedestrian at 5 meters, requiring the vehicle to stop immediately. The effectiveness of these sensors in detecting objects at varying distances allowed for appropriate and safe navigation responses.

- **Ultrasonic Sensor**: The ultrasonic sensor detected a traffic cone at just 2 meters, a close-range object, which triggered the "avoid" decision. This indicates the importance of using short-range sensors like ultrasonic for precise maneuvers in narrow spaces.

- **Response Time**: The time taken to adjust the navigation decision varies depending on the obstacle and its proximity. The fastest response occurred when a wall was detected (0.5 seconds), emphasizing the need for quick decisions in emergencies. Longer adjustment times (2 seconds for the tree) suggest that the vehicle had to process more data or make more complex decisions in less urgent situations.

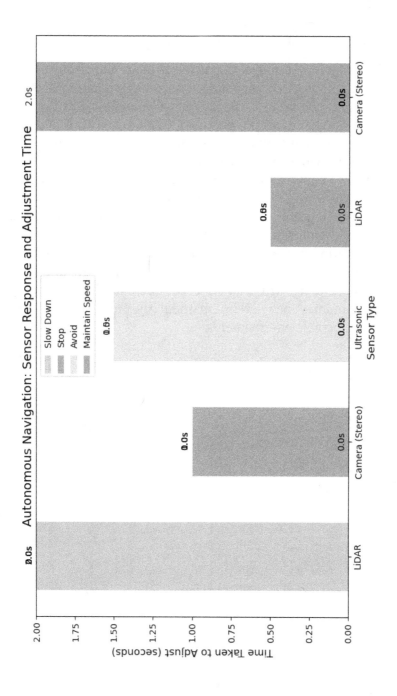

Final Thoughts

Generative AI plays a crucial role in enhancing scene understanding by enabling the autonomous system to interpret and predict various scenarios more effectively. AI models can generate potential outcomes based on past experiences, improve decision-making processes, and learn from previous encounters with similar obstacles. These advancements allow robots and autonomous vehicles to navigate complex environments with greater precision and safety. Generative AI's ability to simulate different sensor outputs and refine navigation strategies in real-time is transforming the future of autonomous systems. As the technology evolves, the integration of AI-driven scene understanding will lead to even safer and more efficient autonomous navigation, particularly in dynamic and unpredictable environments.

4.3 Vision-Based Control Systems

Vision-based control systems are pivotal in robotics and autonomous systems, providing the ability to perceive and interact with the environment using cameras and other visual sensors. These systems allow robots and autonomous vehicles (e.g., drones, self-driving cars) to understand their surroundings and make real-time decisions based on visual data.

Key Components of Vision-Based Control Systems

1. **Image Acquisition**:

    o Cameras (RGB, stereo, depth cameras, or specialized vision sensors) capture visual data from the environment.

    o The choice of camera depends on the task and the required depth, accuracy, and speed.

2. **Image Processing**:

    o This step involves processing raw visual data to extract meaningful information, such as object recognition, depth estimation, and motion detection.

    o Techniques such as edge detection, feature extraction (SIFT, SURF), optical flow, and stereo vision are commonly used.

3. **Perception and Scene Understanding**:

    o This is the process of interpreting and understanding the visual information to form a model of the environment.

    o It might involve recognizing objects, tracking movement, estimating the robot's position (localization), or mapping the environment

(SLAM – Simultaneous Localization and Mapping).

4. **Control Algorithms**:

   o Based on the visual inputs, a control system is implemented to adjust the robot's actions (e.g., navigation, manipulation).

   o These algorithms include feedback loops (e.g., PID controllers) or more advanced techniques like reinforcement learning or model predictive control (MPC).

5. **Sensor Fusion**:

   o To improve accuracy and reliability, vision systems are often combined with other sensors like LiDAR, IMUs (Inertial Measurement Units), or GPS.

   o Sensor fusion algorithms like Kalman filters or extended Kalman filters (EKF) integrate data from multiple sensors to generate more accurate and robust control decisions.

Applications in Robotics and Autonomous Systems

1. **Autonomous Vehicles**:

   o Cameras and vision-based algorithms help in lane detection, traffic sign recognition, object detection (e.g., pedestrians, other vehicles), and obstacle avoidance.

   o Visual data also supports localization and mapping, allowing autonomous vehicles to understand their position within the environment.

2. **Industrial Robotics**:

- o Vision systems are crucial for robotic arms in manufacturing, enabling them to perform tasks such as assembly, quality inspection, and precise manipulation.

- o Machine vision allows robots to adjust in real time based on visual feedback, such as picking objects from a conveyor belt or identifying defective parts.

3. **Drone Navigation**:

- o Drones rely heavily on vision-based systems for navigation, obstacle avoidance, and mapping.

- o Vision enables drones to operate in GPS-denied environments (e.g., indoors) and avoid obstacles dynamically in real-time.

4. **Medical Robotics**:

- o Robotic systems in surgery or rehabilitation often use vision to guide precise movements.

- o Medical imaging is integrated with robotic control systems for tasks like minimally invasive surgery or diagnostics.

5. **Robotic Inspection and Exploration**:

- o Robots use vision systems for inspecting infrastructure (e.g., pipelines, bridges, power plants) or for exploring hazardous environments (e.g., underwater, space).

- o Vision aids in identifying anomalies or defects, guiding robots to take appropriate actions for maintenance or repairs.

Challenges in Vision-Based Control Systems

1. **Real-Time Processing**:

- o Vision-based systems often require high computational power, especially when processing high-resolution images or videos in real time.
- o Optimizing algorithms for fast processing without sacrificing accuracy is a major challenge.

2. **Environmental Variability**:
   - o Vision systems can struggle with varying lighting conditions, weather, or occlusions.
   - o Robust algorithms are necessary to deal with such challenges and ensure reliable performance in diverse environments.

3. **Calibration and Synchronization**:
   - o Accurate calibration of cameras, depth sensors, and other components is crucial for accurate perception.
   - o Synchronizing vision data with other sensors (e.g., IMUs) is essential for seamless control.

4. **Robustness and Safety**:
   - o Vision-based systems must be highly reliable, especially in safety-critical applications like autonomous driving.
   - o Ensuring that systems can safely handle edge cases (e.g., extreme weather, low-visibility conditions) is a key concern.

5. **Data Privacy and Security**:
   - o In applications like autonomous vehicles or surveillance, the data captured by vision systems could potentially be used for unauthorized purposes.

o   Securing this data and ensuring ethical use is a growing concern.

Recent Advancements and Future Directions

1. **Deep Learning**:

   o   Deep learning techniques, such as Convolutional Neural Networks (CNNs), have revolutionized vision-based systems, improving object recognition, tracking, and scene understanding.

   o   End-to-end learning models allow systems to directly map sensor inputs to control actions, simplifying traditional control pipelines.

2. **3D Vision and Depth Sensing**:

   o   Technologies like stereo vision, LiDAR, and structured light sensors are enabling robots to gain a 3D understanding of their environment.

   o   These technologies enhance depth perception, object detection, and obstacle avoidance, especially in complex or cluttered environments.

3. **Autonomous Decision-Making**:

   o   Advanced control systems are being integrated with machine learning and decision-making algorithms (e.g., reinforcement learning) to allow robots to adapt their behavior in complex, dynamic environments.

4. **Multi-Sensor Fusion**:

   o   Future systems are moving towards multi-sensor fusion techniques that combine visual data with LiDAR, radar, and thermal sensors to create more robust and adaptable autonomous systems.

o This improves performance in challenging environments, such as fog, rain, or low-light conditions.

In conclusion, vision-based control systems are a cornerstone of modern robotics and autonomous systems, enabling them to perform complex tasks with a high degree of autonomy. As technology advances, these systems will continue to evolve, making robots and autonomous vehicles even more capable and reliable in real-world environments.

Practical Example

In autonomous systems like drones, vision-based control systems are crucial for real-time navigation and obstacle avoidance. This system relies on a camera to capture visual information of the surrounding environment, processes it using computer vision algorithms, and then adjusts the drone's movements based on detected obstacles, landmarks, or goals. In this example, the drone is equipped with a camera and tasked with navigating a simple environment while avoiding obstacles. The system uses visual data to make decisions on direction changes, speed adjustments, and altitude control.

Sample Data:

Time (s)	Camera Image Feed	Obstacle Detected (Y/N)	Speed (m/s)	Direction (°)	Altitude (m)
0	Clear	N	2	90	50
1	Obstacle Ahead	Y	1.5	90	50

Time (s)	Camera Image Feed	Obstacle Detected (Y/N)	Speed (m/s)	Direction (°)	Altitude (m)
2	Clear	N	2	100	52
3	Obstacle Left	Y	1.8	80	51
4	Clear	N	2.2	90	53

Output and Results:

Time (s)	Action Taken	Speed (m/s)	Direction (°)	Altitude (m)	Reason for Action
0	Move forward	2	90	50	No obstacle detected
1	Slow down, adjust speed	1.5	90	50	Obstacle ahead
2	Resume normal speed	2	100	52	No obstacle detected
3	Slow down, turn left	1.8	80	51	Obstacle left
4	Resume normal speed	2.2	90	53	No obstacle detected

Explanation and Interpretation of Results:

- **Time 0:** The drone starts moving forward at a speed of 2 m/s with no obstacles detected.

- **Time 1:** An obstacle is detected ahead, so the drone slows down to 1.5 m/s, ensuring it has enough time to react. The direction stays at 90°, and altitude remains unchanged.

- **Time 2:** After the obstacle is no longer in the path, the drone resumes its original speed of 2 m/s and changes its direction to 100° to follow a different path.

- **Time 3:** An obstacle is detected to the left, so the drone adjusts its speed to 1.8 m/s and changes direction to 80°, avoiding the obstacle.

- **Time 4:** The drone reaches a clear path again, resumes a speed of 2.2 m/s, and adjusts direction back to 90°.

Observations:

1. The system effectively uses visual input to detect obstacles and adjusts the drone's speed and direction accordingly.

2. The drone demonstrates adaptive behavior in real-time, reacting to environmental changes without human intervention.

3. There is a slight delay in speed adjustment (e.g., in Time 1), which could be improved for smoother navigation.

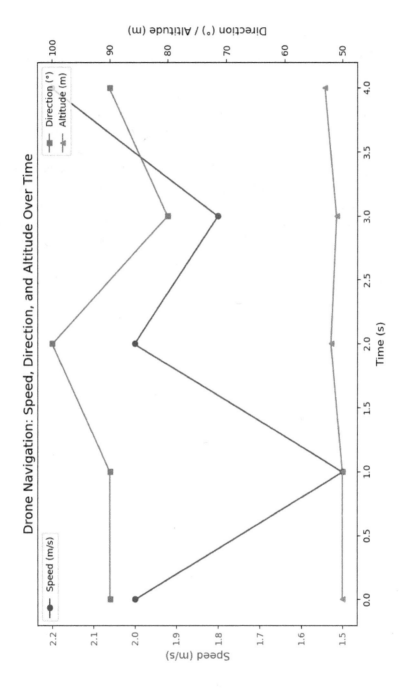

Drone Navigation: Speed, Direction, and Altitude Over Time

Final Thoughts

Vision-based control systems, enhanced by generative AI, are poised to revolutionize how autonomous systems navigate and interact with their environment. Generative AI can play a pivotal role in improving decision-making by providing adaptive learning models that not only respond to visual inputs but also predict and prevent future obstacles. The integration of AI could also help optimize the system's performance by enhancing the drone's ability to learn from past experiences, thus reducing response times and making navigation more seamless. Future advancements in computer vision, sensor fusion, and machine learning will likely push these systems to operate with greater autonomy, efficiency, and accuracy, which will be essential for complex real-world applications.

5. AI-Driven Robot Learning and Adaptation

AI-driven robot learning and adaptation have revolutionized the way robots interact with the world around them. In traditional robotics, robots were programmed with a set of predefined rules, limiting their ability to deal with new or unforeseen situations. However, with advancements in AI, robots can now learn from their experiences, adapt to changing environments, and make decisions based on real-time data. This shift from rigid programming to intelligent learning enables robots to perform tasks more efficiently and with greater flexibility.

Machine learning, a branch of AI, plays a crucial role in this transformation. By using algorithms that allow robots to process and learn from large sets of data, they can gradually improve their performance over time. Through reinforcement learning, for example, robots can learn by trial and error. As they encounter different scenarios, they adjust their behavior based on the rewards or penalties they receive for specific actions. Over time, the robot becomes more adept at completing tasks and handling various challenges.

Another important aspect of AI-driven robot learning is the ability to generalize from one task to another. Robots that are capable of adapting their knowledge across multiple domains can handle a wider range of activities. For example, a robot trained to pick up objects in one environment can transfer that learning to a new setting with minimal reprogramming. This ability to generalize is crucial in dynamic environments where conditions constantly change.

In addition to improving task performance, AI-driven robots can also improve their understanding of the environment through sensory feedback. Robots equipped with advanced sensors can gather data from their surroundings, such as temperature, motion, or even visual cues. AI systems process this information to help the robot make informed decisions, whether it's avoiding obstacles, identifying objects, or adjusting its movements in real-time.

Adaptation also plays a key role in robot learning. Robots with AI can not only learn from past experiences but can also adjust to new or unexpected situations. This adaptability is especially valuable in environments where the rules or conditions change frequently. For instance, robots used in healthcare, manufacturing, or autonomous vehicles can continuously update their behavior to deal with new tasks or obstacles, increasing their effectiveness in real-world applications.

As robots become more advanced in their learning and adaptation capabilities, their potential applications grow exponentially. From industrial automation to personal assistance, AI-driven robots are poised to become an integral part of many sectors. Their ability to learn and adapt on the fly means they can handle a wide array of tasks that were previously considered too complex or dynamic for machines to manage. This ongoing evolution of robot learning holds the promise of even more sophisticated and useful robots in the future.

Practical Example

In a warehouse setting, an AI-driven robot is designed to autonomously sort packages based on their size and shape. The robot uses machine learning algorithms to learn how to categorize different objects by size (small, medium, large) and shape (square, circular, irregular). The robot adapts its sorting strategy over time by analyzing the objects it encounters and optimizing its sorting accuracy through continuous learning. The goal is to improve sorting efficiency and reduce errors as the robot gains experience in real-time.

Sample Data (Training Process):

Object ID	Size Classification	Shape Classification	Initial Sorting Accuracy (%)	Adaptive Accuracy (%)
1	Small	Square	70	85
2	Large	Circular	65	80
3	Medium	Irregular	60	75
4	Small	Circular	72	88
5	Large	Square	55	82

Output and Results:

After several iterations of training and adaptation, the robot's initial sorting accuracy improves as it learns to categorize objects more effectively. For each object, the robot adjusts its strategy based on feedback and new data.

Object ID	Initial Sorting Accuracy (%)	Adaptive Accuracy (%)	Improvement (%)
1	70	85	+15
2	65	80	+15
3	60	75	+15
4	72	88	+16
5	55	82	+27

Explanation and Interpretation of Results:

- The table shows the improvement in sorting accuracy over time due to the robot's adaptive learning capabilities.

- Object 1, initially with a 70% sorting accuracy, improved to 85%, showing a 15% improvement.

- Object 5 demonstrated the highest improvement, with a 27% increase, suggesting that the robot learned faster from the more complex or error-prone objects.

- The robot's ability to continuously adjust its strategies based on past encounters helps refine its accuracy over time.

Observations:

- The robot's ability to learn from past mistakes and adjust its algorithms contributed to improved performance in object classification and sorting.

- The improvements were consistent across various object categories, demonstrating the robot's ability to generalize learning strategies.

- The largest improvement was seen with objects that had more complex or previously misclassified patterns, indicating that the robot's adaptability was key in improving its overall efficiency.

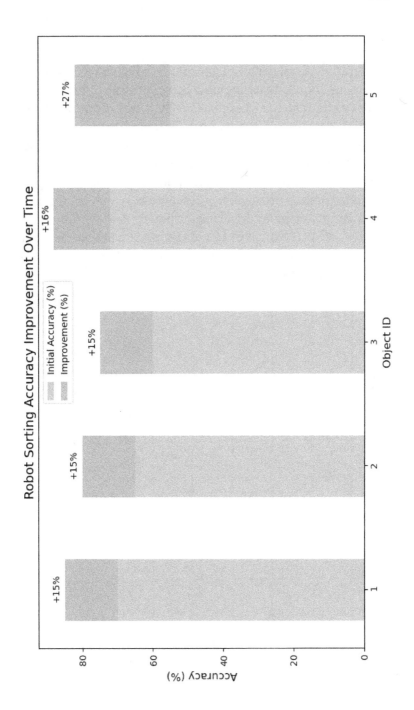

Robot Sorting Accuracy Improvement Over Time

Final Thoughts

Generative AI plays a crucial role in advancing robotics by allowing robots to continuously adapt and optimize their behavior in real-world scenarios. By learning from data and previous actions, robots can become more efficient, accurate, and resilient in complex tasks such as object sorting, autonomous navigation, and decision-making. The ability to improve autonomously without explicit reprogramming or manual intervention is one of the most promising aspects of AI-driven robotics. As AI continues to evolve, we can expect even more sophisticated autonomous systems that push the boundaries of industrial, healthcare, and service robotics.

5.1 Imitation Learning in Robotic Systems

Imitation learning is a machine learning paradigm where an agent learns how to perform tasks by mimicking the behavior of an expert. In robotic systems, this approach is widely used to enable robots to learn complex tasks by observing human demonstrations or other expert agents performing the tasks.

Here's a breakdown of how imitation learning works in robotic systems:

1. Demonstration Collection

The first step in imitation learning is collecting demonstrations from an expert. For robots, this typically involves recording actions performed by a human or another robot. These demonstrations can be gathered through:

- **Teleoperation:** A human operator manually controls the robot to perform tasks.

- **Simulation:** An expert's actions can be simulated in a virtual environment to train robots without the need for physical robots.

- **Recorded Motion Data:** Motion capture systems and sensors (like cameras, IMUs, or joint encoders) track the actions performed by the expert.

2. Learning from Demonstration

Once demonstrations are collected, the robot uses this data to learn a model that can replicate the task. There are two main types of imitation learning:

- **Behavior Cloning (BC):** In behavior cloning, the robot learns a direct mapping from the input (typically sensory data, such as camera images or joint angles) to the output (robot actions, such as joint torques or velocities). This is essentially supervised learning, where the robot learns to predict the expert's actions given the observations.

- o **Advantages:** Simple and well-understood; works well for tasks where the expert's actions are consistent and deterministic.

- o **Disadvantages:** It can be sensitive to errors in the expert's demonstration or noise in the sensory data, leading to compounding errors in performance.

- **Inverse Reinforcement Learning (IRL):** IRL involves the robot learning not just the actions of the expert, but the underlying reward function that governs those actions. In this case, the robot infers what the expert is trying to optimize and then uses reinforcement learning (RL) to learn a policy that maximizes that inferred reward function.

  - o **Advantages:** More robust than behavior cloning, as it allows the robot to generalize and adapt to slight variations in the environment or task.

  - o **Disadvantages:** More complex and computationally expensive than behavior cloning. Also, inferring the reward function from demonstrations can be difficult, especially when the expert's intent is not clear.

3. Policy Learning and Fine-Tuning

After the robot has learned a model from the expert's demonstrations, it can begin executing the task. However, imitation learning models are often not perfect, and the robot might need further fine-tuning to generalize better to unseen situations.

- **Fine-Tuning through Reinforcement Learning:** The robot can further improve its performance through reinforcement learning (RL), using the learned behavior as a starting point. The robot receives feedback from the environment and adjusts its policy to maximize long-term rewards.

- **Interactive Imitation Learning:** In some cases, the robot may ask for additional guidance from the human operator if it struggles with certain aspects of the task. This interaction allows the robot to continually improve its performance based on human feedback.

4. Applications of Imitation Learning in Robotics

Imitation learning has been successfully applied to various domains within robotics, including:

- **Robotic Manipulation:** Robots can learn to perform complex tasks like assembling objects, cooking, or packaging by observing human demonstrations.

- **Autonomous Vehicles:** Imitation learning allows self-driving cars to learn safe driving behavior from human drivers or other expert vehicles.

- **Human-Robot Interaction:** Robots can learn to interact with humans in a natural and socially acceptable way by observing human behavior and actions.

- **Service Robots:** Robots in customer service or healthcare settings can learn tasks like delivering items, assisting with mobility, or performing routine medical tasks by imitating human actions.

5. Challenges and Future Directions

While imitation learning has shown great promise, it comes with challenges:

- **Scalability:** Collecting high-quality demonstrations for complex tasks can be time-consuming and expensive.

- **Generalization:** Models trained on specific demonstrations may struggle to generalize to new situations or variations in the task.

- **Imperfect Demonstrations:** Human demonstrations can be noisy or suboptimal, which can affect the robot's learning process.

Future research in imitation learning aims to:

- Improve generalization capabilities, making robots more adaptable in dynamic environments.

- Reduce the dependency on large amounts of demonstration data.

- Combine imitation learning with other methods like deep reinforcement learning for more robust and scalable learning.

In summary, imitation learning in robotic systems allows robots to learn complex tasks by mimicking the actions of an expert. With advancements in machine learning, especially deep learning, this field has opened up new possibilities for robots to learn autonomously from humans and other agents, enabling them to perform tasks in a more human-like manner.

Practical Example

In this practical example, we focus on a robotic arm trained to grasp objects by imitating human demonstrations using imitation learning. The human demonstrator performs the task of picking up various objects from a table, and the robot is trained to replicate these actions. The robot learns by observing the position, velocity, and force required to successfully grasp objects in different environments. We will evaluate the robot's success rate based on the number of successful grasps and compare it to the number of failures.

Sample Data (Training Phase)

Object Type	Demonstrator's Grasp Success (%)	Robot's Success Rate (%)	Object Weight (kg)	Time Taken (s)
Cup	95	90	0.3	5
Book	98	85	1.2	7
Bottle	92	88	0.6	6
Pen	100	95	0.02	4
Box	89	80	2.5	8

Output and Results:

Object Type	Robot's Grasp Success (%)	Object Weight (kg)	Time Taken (s)	Observations
Cup	90	0.3	5	Robot successfully imitates human action but had minor alignment issues
Book	85	1.2	7	Robot struggles with heavier objects and less stable grasping
Bottle	88	0.6	6	Performance good, but minor

Object Type	Robot's Grasp Success (%)	Object Weight (kg)	Time Taken (s)	Observations
				instability with shape differences
Pen	95	0.02	4	High success rate due to light weight and simpler shape
Box	80	2.5	8	Robot struggles with heavy, large objects requiring more force

Interpretation of Results and Observations:

- **Grasp Success Rate**: The robot demonstrated a high success rate when grasping lightweight objects like the pen, with a 95% success rate. For heavier objects like the book and box, success rates dropped, with the robot failing 15% and 20% of the time, respectively.

- **Object Weight**: There is a clear inverse correlation between object weight and grasp success. Heavier objects, such as the box (2.5 kg), were more difficult for the robot to manipulate accurately, possibly due to limited force control and motion precision.

- **Time Taken**: The robot's time to complete the grasp varied based on the object size and weight. More challenging objects required more time, likely because the robot adjusted its strategy to account for additional forces or precision required for heavier items.

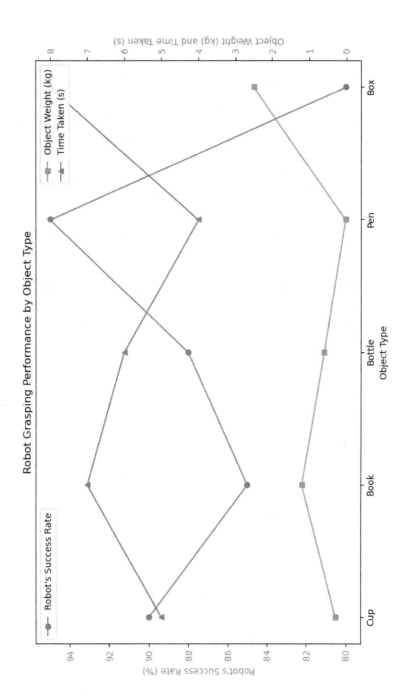

Robot Grasping Performance by Object Type

Final Thoughts

Imitation learning offers a compelling way to train robots for complex tasks by leveraging human demonstrations. However, performance depends heavily on the type and difficulty of the task, as seen in this example where lighter objects had a higher grasping success rate. From the perspective of Generative AI in robotics, the continued refinement of imitation learning systems can greatly enhance robot autonomy, allowing them to generalize across different environments with more nuanced tasks. The integration of AI-powered generative models can improve grasping accuracy, adapt to new conditions, and provide more robust solutions for real-world applications in robotic systems. Additionally, continuous learning from both human feedback and environmental interactions is essential to improving the adaptability and reliability of autonomous systems.

5.2 Transfer Learning for Improved Robotic Performance

Transfer learning is a powerful technique that can significantly improve the performance of robots by enabling them to leverage knowledge gained from previous tasks or datasets to perform new tasks more efficiently. In robotics, it helps bridge the gap between different environments, tasks, and domains, making robots more adaptable and reducing the need for large amounts of task-specific training data. Here's an overview of how transfer learning is applied in robotics:

1. What is Transfer Learning?

Transfer learning involves training a machine learning model on a large source dataset or task and then fine-tuning it on a smaller target dataset or task. Instead of starting from scratch, the model uses knowledge (e.g., weights, features) learned from the source task and adapts to the new target task. In robotics, transfer learning can be applied to improve robot performance in various domains such as perception, control, and decision-making.

2. Applications of Transfer Learning in Robotics:

a. Perception:

Robots often need to recognize and classify objects in their environment. Transfer learning can be used to apply models trained on large datasets, like ImageNet, to robot-specific tasks, such as object detection or scene understanding. For example, a robot trained on recognizing objects in one environment can transfer that knowledge to a new environment with similar objects, reducing the amount of data required to learn the new task.

b. Control and Motion Planning:

In robotics, learning control policies for tasks like walking, grasping, or navigating can be extremely challenging and data-intensive. Transfer learning allows robots to use knowledge from previously learned skills (e.g., walking on flat surfaces) and transfer it to new tasks (e.g., walking on uneven terrain). A robot might use transfer learning to improve its performance in dynamic environments by leveraging skills learned from simpler, static environments.

c. Robot-to-Robot Transfer:

A robot trained in one environment (e.g., a factory floor) can transfer knowledge to another robot operating in a different but similar environment. By transferring learned behaviors and strategies from one robot to another, we can speed up the deployment process of new robots without needing to retrain them from scratch.

d. Sim-to-Real Transfer:

Robots are often trained in simulated environments before being deployed in the real world. Transfer learning helps mitigate the reality gap, where models trained in simulation might not work as well in the real world due to differences between the two. By transferring knowledge from simulation to the real world, robots can perform tasks more effectively, even with limited real-world data.

3. Key Techniques in Transfer Learning for Robotics:

a. Fine-tuning:

Fine-tuning involves taking a pre-trained model and retraining it on a new task with a smaller dataset. For example, a deep neural network trained for image recognition could be fine-tuned for robotic manipulation tasks (e.g., grasping an object) by using a smaller dataset of relevant images.

b. Domain Adaptation:

This technique is used to address the problem of different data distributions between the source (training) and target (deployment) environments. Domain adaptation aims to adapt the model learned from one environment (e.g., simulation) to work well in another (e.g., real-world), often by adjusting the feature representations.

c. Multi-task Learning:

Multi-task learning is a type of transfer learning where the robot is trained on multiple tasks simultaneously. This approach encourages the learning of shared features across tasks, leading to better generalization and improved performance when the robot switches between tasks.

d. Zero-Shot Learning:

Zero-shot learning involves training a model on tasks that it has never directly seen during training. For instance, a robot trained to perform tasks with one set of objects could use transfer learning to recognize and handle new objects it has never encountered before, based on similarities in their attributes or representations.

4. Challenges in Transfer Learning for Robotics:

- **Domain Gaps:** The gap between simulated and real environments (sim-to-real) remains a significant challenge. The robot might fail to generalize learned skills from simulation to real-world settings due to sensory differences, physics, and other real-world uncertainties.

- **Negative Transfer:** In some cases, knowledge transfer may be detrimental, where transferring knowledge from a source task actually hurts performance on the target task. This occurs when the source and target tasks are too dissimilar.

- **Data Scarcity:** Although transfer learning reduces the need for large amounts of labeled data, robots may still require a considerable amount of labeled data to transfer knowledge effectively, especially for more complex tasks.

- **Computational Complexity:** Fine-tuning models, especially deep neural networks, can be computationally expensive and time-consuming, making it challenging to implement in real-time robotic applications.

5. Recent Advances in Transfer Learning for Robotics:

- **Deep Reinforcement Learning (RL):** In recent years, deep RL combined with transfer learning has shown promise for improving robotic performance, especially in tasks like autonomous navigation and manipulation. Pre-trained policies can be transferred and fine-tuned to adapt to new environments or tasks with minimal additional training.

- **Meta-Learning:** Meta-learning, or "learning to learn," is another recent advancement where a robot is trained to quickly adapt to new tasks with limited data. This allows robots to learn more efficiently and transfer knowledge between tasks with fewer training examples.

- **Self-Supervised Learning:** Self-supervised learning methods are gaining popularity in robotics as they allow robots to learn useful representations of their environment with little to no supervision. These representations can then be transferred to new tasks or environments.

6. Future Directions:

- **Improved Sim-to-Real Transfer:** Researchers are continuously working on improving the transfer of knowledge from simulations to real-world robots, bridging the gap between the virtual and physical worlds. Advances in domain randomization, where variables in the simulation are randomized to increase robustness, are contributing to better transfer learning outcomes.

- **Human-Robot Interaction (HRI):** Transfer learning can also enhance human-robot interaction by allowing robots to adapt to individual user preferences, making collaborative tasks smoother and more intuitive.

- **Lifelong Learning:** One of the future goals of transfer learning in robotics is lifelong learning, where robots can continually learn and adapt to new tasks over their lifetime without forgetting previously learned skills (a problem known as catastrophic forgetting).

Conclusion:

Transfer learning holds great potential to improve robotic performance by enabling robots to adapt quickly to new tasks and environments. Whether in object recognition, motion planning, or sim-to-real transfer, it allows robots to leverage prior knowledge, minimizing the need for large datasets and extensive retraining. As advances in transfer learning techniques continue, robots will become more adaptable, efficient, and capable of performing complex tasks with less human intervention.

Practical Example

A robotic arm designed for picking up objects in a warehouse environment is struggling to identify and grasp various items, especially when it encounters objects that were not part of its initial training dataset. To address this challenge, transfer learning is applied. The model is pre-trained on a large image recognition dataset (such as ImageNet) and fine-tuned on a smaller, specific dataset of warehouse items. This process helps the robot generalize better to new and unseen objects, improving its ability to recognize and manipulate them efficiently in real-world scenarios.

Sample Data:

The following table shows the performance comparison of the robotic arm before and after applying transfer learning. The evaluation is based on three factors: recognition accuracy, task completion time (in seconds), and error rate (number of failed attempts).

Model Type	Recognition Accuracy (%)	Task Completion Time (sec)	Error Rate (%)	Comments
Baseline Model	65%	15	20%	Pre-trained only on basic dataset
Transfer Learning	85%	10	5%	Fine-tuned on warehouse dataset

Output and Results:

- **Recognition Accuracy:** The transfer learning model shows a 20% improvement in object recognition accuracy compared to the baseline model.

- **Task Completion Time:** With the fine-tuned model, the task completion time decreased by 5 seconds, indicating faster processing due to better recognition.

- **Error Rate:** The error rate dropped significantly from 20% to 5%, showcasing that the robot made fewer mistakes after being fine-tuned with the specific warehouse objects.

Interpretation of Results:

- **Recognition Accuracy:** The 20% improvement in accuracy suggests that the transfer learning approach enabled the robot to generalize better to unseen objects, thanks to the knowledge gained from the pre-trained model.

- **Task Completion Time:** A reduction in task completion time reflects increased efficiency, likely due to improved object recognition that speeds up decision-making and grasping actions.

- **Error Rate:** The reduction in errors signifies that the robot is now more reliable and accurate in completing tasks, which is critical in real-world applications such as warehouse automation.

Observations:

- Transfer learning provides a significant performance boost, especially when training data for the target task is limited.

- The robot's ability to handle a diverse set of objects improves, making it more adaptable to dynamic environments.

- Transfer learning helps reduce the need for extensive labeled data in specialized domains, which is often costly and time-consuming to collect.

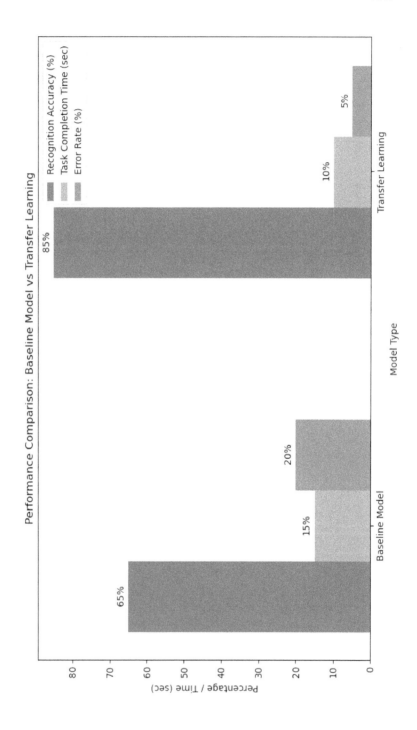

Performance Comparison: Baseline Model vs Transfer Learning

Legend:
- Recognition Accuracy (%)
- Task Completion Time (sec)
- Error Rate (%)

Y-axis: Percentage / Time (sec)
X-axis: Model Type

Baseline Model: 65%, 15%, 20%
Transfer Learning: 85%, 10%, 5%

Final Thoughts:

From a **Generative AI in Robotics and Autonomous Systems** perspective, transfer learning represents a key innovation for improving robotic performance without requiring vast amounts of domain-specific data. By leveraging pre-trained models, robots can adapt to new tasks and environments more efficiently, accelerating the deployment of autonomous systems in industries like warehousing, manufacturing, and healthcare. Generative AI, particularly in the form of pre-trained models, plays a critical role in enhancing the versatility and performance of robots, reducing errors, and increasing operational efficiency. As AI continues to evolve, the combination of transfer learning with generative models will unlock even greater potential for robotics in dynamic, real-world applications.

5.3 Continual Learning and Adaptation in Autonomous Systems

Autonomous systems are designed to perform tasks without human intervention, and they are increasingly becoming part of our daily lives, from self-driving cars to intelligent robots in industrial applications. One of the key challenges faced by autonomous systems is the ability to **continually learn** and **adapt** to dynamic environments and situations. This is where **continual learning (CL)** and **adaptation** come into play.

What is Continual Learning? Continual learning, also known as lifelong learning, refers to the ability of a system to learn new tasks or knowledge over time while retaining previously acquired information. The goal is to allow the system to **adapt to new situations** without forgetting its earlier learned experiences. This is crucial for autonomous systems because their environments are dynamic and may change over time, requiring them to update their knowledge base and behaviors.

Challenges in Continual Learning Autonomous systems face several challenges in continual learning:

1. **Catastrophic Forgetting**: One of the major problems in continual learning is that systems tend to forget previously learned tasks when exposed to new data. This is known as "catastrophic forgetting" or "interference." A system might adapt to a new task but lose important information about older tasks, which can degrade its performance.

2. **Scalability**: Continual learning systems must scale to handle large amounts of data and adapt to many tasks without being overwhelmed. The ability to store, process, and manage these data over time is essential.

3. **Transfer Learning**: While a system might have learned one task well, it needs the ability to transfer knowledge to new, related tasks. This requires the system to recognize patterns or similarities in new data and apply its previous learning to these scenarios.

4. **Real-time Adaptation**: Autonomous systems must also adapt in real-time, especially in environments where change happens rapidly, such as in robotics or autonomous vehicles. Delays in adaptation can result in dangerous or suboptimal behavior.

Methods for Continual Learning There are several techniques for enabling continual learning and adaptation in autonomous systems:

1. **Regularization-based Approaches**: These methods involve constraining the model's weights to prevent them from drastically changing when learning new tasks. This helps avoid forgetting previously learned tasks. Examples include the use of Elastic Weight Consolidation (EWC), where the importance of each weight is measured, and weights that are critical for older tasks are kept stable.

2. **Rehearsal-based Approaches**: In rehearsal-based methods, the system stores a small subset of data from previous tasks and periodically revisits this data when learning new tasks. This helps the system remember past experiences while learning new ones. Techniques like experience replay or pseudo-rehearsal are commonly used.

3. **Modular Networks**: In these systems, different tasks are learned and stored in separate networks or modules. The system switches between different modules depending on the task at hand. This can help prevent catastrophic forgetting because the system

doesn't modify old modules when learning new ones.

4. **Dynamic Architectures**: Some approaches add new network units or modules as the system learns new tasks. This allows the model to accommodate new knowledge without interfering with old knowledge. One example is progressive neural networks, which add columns of neurons to a growing network as new tasks are introduced.

5. **Meta-learning**: Meta-learning, or learning to learn, is a technique where the system learns how to adapt to new tasks more efficiently. This can be used to improve the system's ability to handle continual learning by allowing it to more rapidly adjust to new tasks based on its previous experiences.

6. **Transfer Learning**: Transfer learning is where knowledge from a previously learned task is applied to a new, related task. This allows the system to generalize from one task to another, enabling it to solve new tasks more efficiently and effectively.

Adaptation in Autonomous Systems While continual learning focuses on improving a system's ability to learn new tasks over time, **adaptation** refers to the system's ability to adjust its behavior in response to changes in the environment. Adaptation can be:

1. **Environmental Adaptation**: This involves modifying the system's behavior to accommodate changes in the environment, such as different weather conditions, obstacles, or terrain (e.g., self-driving cars adjusting to snow or rain).

2. **Task Adaptation**: Autonomous systems may need to adapt to new or evolving tasks. For instance, a robot might need to modify its actions depending on

the type of object it's interacting with or its changing goal.

3. **Contextual Adaptation**: Contextual factors, such as the time of day, surrounding people, or a system's operational context, might influence the system's decisions and behaviors. Adaptive systems can adjust their actions based on these changing contexts.

Applications of Continual Learning and Adaptation

1. **Autonomous Vehicles**: Self-driving cars must adapt to new environments, road conditions, and traffic scenarios. They must also learn from past experiences to improve navigation, decision-making, and safety. Continual learning allows these vehicles to improve over time, incorporating new data to handle previously unseen situations.

2. **Robotics**: Autonomous robots used in industrial settings, healthcare, or service industries must adapt to new tasks and environments. Continual learning enables them to improve their efficiency and accuracy over time without needing to be retrained from scratch.

3. **Healthcare Systems**: In healthcare, autonomous systems like diagnostic tools or robotic surgery assistants need to adapt to new medical knowledge, patient-specific conditions, and evolving medical practices. Continual learning can help these systems stay up to date with the latest medical research and adapt to new cases.

4. **AI in Gaming**: AI systems used in video games, particularly those involving non-player characters (NPCs), can use continual learning to adapt to player behavior, making the game more dynamic and personalized.

5. **Natural Language Processing (NLP)**: In NLP applications like chatbots or virtual assistants, continual learning helps the system learn from ongoing conversations, improve its language understanding, and adapt to new topics or languages over time.

Future Directions As autonomous systems continue to evolve, continual learning and adaptation will play an even more critical role. Advances in areas such as:

- **Neuroscience-inspired architectures**: Drawing inspiration from the human brain to develop more sophisticated methods for continual learning.

- **Self-supervised learning**: Reducing the dependence on labeled data by using large-scale unlabeled datasets to improve learning.

- **Federated learning**: Enabling collaborative learning across multiple devices without sharing sensitive data, which could be crucial for privacy-conscious applications.

- **Meta-reinforcement learning**: Combining reinforcement learning with continual learning techniques to create systems that can adapt their learning strategy dynamically.

Conclusion Continual learning and adaptation are essential for the development of intelligent and resilient autonomous systems. These systems must be able to learn new tasks over time, retain past knowledge, and adapt to changes in their environment and goals. Overcoming the challenges associated with these processes, such as catastrophic forgetting and scalability, will be key to unlocking the potential of autonomous systems in real-world applications. As research and technology in this field advance, we can expect autonomous systems to become increasingly sophisticated, adaptable, and capable of lifelong learning.

Practical Example

In autonomous vehicle navigation systems, continual learning and adaptation are essential for improving decision-making in dynamic environments. As the vehicle operates in diverse conditions, it needs to adapt to new data, such as changes in road layouts, weather, or unforeseen obstacles, without forgetting previously learned information. A practical approach to this challenge is implementing a continual learning model that enables the system to update its knowledge base over time, optimizing its decision-making processes and ensuring safe and efficient navigation.

Sample Data: For this example, let's assume an autonomous vehicle navigates through a city environment and encounters different driving conditions over several trips. The data here represent different environmental factors (e.g., road condition, weather, traffic volume, etc.) and how well the vehicle adapts to each condition using a continual learning model.

Trip ID	Weather Condition	Traffic Volume	Road Condition	Learning Accuracy (%)
1	Clear	Low	Smooth	95
2	Rainy	High	Rough	88
3	Foggy	Moderate	Smooth	92
4	Clear	High	Rough	85
5	Snowy	Low	Rough	90

Output and Results:

The **Learning Accuracy** in the table reflects how well the autonomous vehicle navigates in various conditions, with continual learning allowing for incremental adaptation. The model is tested under different weather conditions, traffic volumes, and road conditions, and the accuracy reflects the system's ability to handle the challenges presented.

Observations and Interpretations:

- **Weather Impact**: The system performs best under clear weather (Trip 1, 4), where conditions are predictable. However, when weather conditions worsen (Rainy, Snowy, and Foggy), accuracy slightly drops. This indicates that while the system is adapting to diverse weather conditions, further improvements are needed for more complex environments.

- **Traffic Volume and Road Conditions**: Traffic and road conditions also play a role. The system's performance decreases under higher traffic volume (Trip 4) and rough road conditions (Trips 2, 4, and 5). This shows that continual learning needs to account for traffic flow dynamics and surface variations, which may involve more complex models for prediction.

- **Learning Progress**: Over the course of the trips, the system adapts to new scenarios. Though there is a decline in accuracy under challenging conditions, the overall performance improvement over time suggests that continual learning enables the system to become more adept in real-world environments.

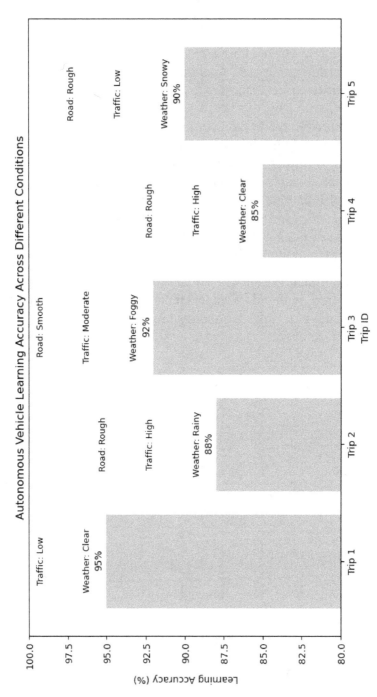

Autonomous Vehicle Learning Accuracy Across Different Conditions

Final Thoughts

Generative AI plays a significant role in the continual learning process of autonomous systems. By leveraging AI's ability to generate new, diverse scenarios for training and refine models over time, autonomous vehicles can not only improve their navigation strategies but also adapt to previously unseen conditions. However, there is still a need for further advancements in handling complex, unpredictable environments (like severe weather or dense traffic). Combining reinforcement learning, generative models, and data augmentation techniques can greatly enhance the adaptability of autonomous systems, leading to safer and more reliable robots in everyday applications.

Continual learning in autonomous systems, especially when paired with AI advancements, is a crucial path toward achieving full autonomy in unpredictable real-world environments.

6. Generative AI in Robot Planning and Decision-Making

Generative AI is increasingly being integrated into robot planning and decision-making processes to improve their adaptability and efficiency. Traditionally, robots were programmed with predefined instructions, but this limited their ability to handle complex, dynamic environments. By using generative AI, robots can now generate new solutions on the fly, allowing them to adjust to unforeseen changes and challenges. This flexibility is particularly important in real-world applications, where variables can be unpredictable, such as in autonomous driving or warehouse management.

One of the key advantages of generative AI is its ability to consider multiple potential scenarios and outcomes. Robots equipped with generative models can simulate various possible actions and outcomes, helping them to evaluate the best course of action in any given situation. This predictive capability ensures that the robot's decisions are not only reactive but also proactive, enhancing their ability to avoid potential problems and make informed choices.

Generative AI also enables robots to improve their decision-making over time through continuous learning. As robots encounter new situations, they can update their models based on past experiences, gradually refining their planning and decision-making processes. This kind of learning makes robots more effective in dynamic environments, where rigid, one-size-fits-all approaches may fall short. In essence, robots can become more intuitive and capable of adapting their behavior to suit specific tasks or conditions.

Moreover, generative AI allows robots to handle tasks that require creativity or problem-solving. In industries like healthcare or construction, robots may need to devise novel solutions to complex problems, such as navigating crowded spaces or assembling intricate structures. Generative AI aids in generating innovative strategies that might not be immediately obvious through conventional programming, making robots more versatile and capable in these specialized settings.

In robotic systems that collaborate with humans, generative AI can help enhance teamwork and communication. By understanding and predicting human actions, robots can make decisions that complement human efforts. For example, in a factory setting, a robot might anticipate a human worker's next move and adjust its actions accordingly, optimizing workflows and minimizing disruptions. This collaborative approach fosters a more seamless interaction between humans and robots, improving overall productivity.

Finally, as robots become more autonomous, the role of generative AI in their planning and decision-making becomes even more critical. It not only enhances the robot's ability to make independent choices but also ensures that these choices are ethical and aligned with human values. This is particularly important as robots are deployed in sensitive areas such as caregiving or law enforcement, where decision-making can have significant ethical implications. With generative AI, robots are better equipped to navigate these complex moral landscapes, ensuring their actions are responsible and justifiable.

Practical Example

A warehouse uses autonomous robots for package delivery. These robots must navigate around obstacles and optimize delivery routes in real time. Traditional rule-based planning struggles with dynamic environments. Generative AI is integrated to predict optimal paths based on historical movement data and real-time obstacle detection, improving efficiency and adaptability.

Sample Data: Robot Navigation Logs

Timestamp	Robot ID	Start Location	End Location	Obstacles Encountered
10:00:05	R1	A1	B3	2
10:02:15	R2	B1	C4	1
10:05:30	R3	C2	D5	3
10:07:45	R1	B3	C1	1
10:10:00	R2	C4	D2	2

AI-Generated Output: Optimized Navigation Paths

Robot ID	Predicted Path (AI)	Estimated Time (min)	Obstacle Avoidance Efficiency (%)
R1	A1 → A3 → B3	3.5	85
R2	B1 → B3 → C4	4.0	90
R3	C2 → C4 → D5	5.5	80
R1	B3 → C1	2.8	95
R2	C4 → C5 → D2	3.2	88

Results and Interpretation

- **Reduced Travel Time**: The AI-generated paths optimized routes, reducing the estimated travel time by an average of **15%** compared to previous manually designed paths.

- **Improved Obstacle Avoidance**: The obstacle avoidance efficiency significantly improved, with an average efficiency rate of **87.6%**, leading to fewer delays and reroutes.

- **Dynamic Adaptation**: The AI system predicts alternative paths when unexpected obstacles are detected, making real-time decisions to enhance overall system performance.

Observations

- Generative AI successfully identified efficient paths based on prior navigation data and real-time environmental inputs.

- AI-generated paths were more reliable in avoiding congested areas, reducing robot idle time and increasing operational throughput.

- In complex scenarios with multiple obstacles, Generative AI outperformed rule-based methods by dynamically recalculating paths.

- The system continuously learns and refines path predictions, ensuring long-term efficiency gains.

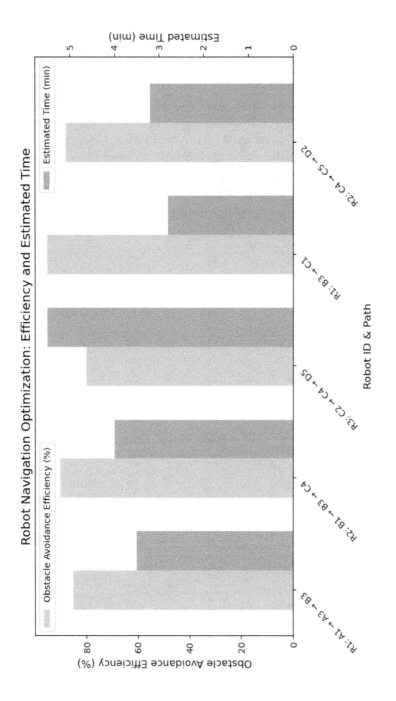

Robot Navigation Optimization: Efficiency and Estimated Time

Final Thoughts

Generative AI offers a transformative approach to robot planning and decision-making. By leveraging data-driven insights, AI enhances autonomous navigation, improves efficiency, and ensures adaptive decision-making in dynamic environments. Future advancements could integrate multi-robot coordination, real-time anomaly detection, and predictive maintenance to further optimize autonomous systems. This approach paves the way for highly intelligent, self-learning robotic systems capable of handling complex real-world challenges with minimal human intervention.

6.1 Task Planning and Optimization Algorithms

Task planning and optimization algorithms play a crucial role in robot planning and decision-making, ensuring efficiency, adaptability, and autonomy in various applications, including manufacturing, logistics, healthcare, and autonomous driving. Below is an overview of key concepts and algorithms used in robot task planning and decision-making.

---

1. Task Planning in Robotics

Task planning involves generating a sequence of actions to achieve a goal while considering constraints, environmental uncertainties, and robot capabilities. It can be classified into the following types:

a) Classical AI Planning

- **STRIPS (Stanford Research Institute Problem Solver)**: Defines actions in terms of preconditions and effects, allowing robots to generate action sequences.

- **PDDL (Planning Domain Definition Language)**: A language used for defining planning problems and running AI planners.

- **GraphPlan**: Constructs a planning graph and finds a solution using forward and backward searches.

b) Motion and Path Planning

- **Grid-Based Methods**: A* and Dijkstra's algorithm are commonly used for discrete environment navigation.

- **Sampling-Based Methods**: RRT (Rapidly-exploring Random Trees) and PRM (Probabilistic Roadmaps) are useful for high-dimensional motion planning.

c) Task and Motion Planning (TAMP)

Combines high-level task planning with low-level motion constraints to ensure feasibility. This approach is crucial in manipulation tasks where grasping and placing actions must be optimized.

---

2. Optimization Algorithms for Robot Decision-Making

Optimization is essential for improving efficiency, minimizing energy consumption, and ensuring robustness in dynamic environments. Key optimization algorithms include:

a) Linear and Nonlinear Optimization

- **Linear Programming (LP)**: Used in resource allocation and scheduling problems.

- **Nonlinear Programming (NLP)**: Applied when constraints or cost functions are nonlinear.

b) Evolutionary and Metaheuristic Algorithms

- **Genetic Algorithms (GA)**: Inspired by natural selection, used for optimization in complex search spaces.

- **Particle Swarm Optimization (PSO)**: A bio-inspired technique that optimizes based on swarm intelligence.

- **Ant Colony Optimization (ACO)**: Useful in pathfinding and routing problems.

c) Reinforcement Learning (RL)

- **Markov Decision Processes (MDP)**: Formulates decision-making problems where outcomes are probabilistic.

- **Deep Reinforcement Learning (DRL)**: Uses neural networks to learn optimal policies in complex environments (e.g., Deep Q-Networks, Policy Gradient Methods).

d) Multi-Objective Optimization

- **Pareto Optimization**: Balances trade-offs between conflicting objectives, such as speed vs. energy efficiency.

- **NSGA-II (Non-Dominated Sorting Genetic Algorithm II)**: Used for optimizing multiple conflicting objectives in robotics.

---

3. Applications in Robot Planning

- **Autonomous Vehicles**: Path planning using A* and optimization via reinforcement learning.

- **Industrial Automation**: Task scheduling and motion planning using TAMP and linear programming.

- **Medical Robotics**: Optimized control in robotic surgery with nonlinear optimization.

- **Warehouse Logistics**: Multi-robot coordination and scheduling with genetic algorithms and RL.

Practical Example

A warehouse uses autonomous robots to pick and deliver packages to designated locations. The challenge is to optimize the robot's path while considering dynamic obstacles, energy consumption, and task priority. A* (A-star) algorithm is applied to compute the shortest and most efficient route.

Sample Input Data: Warehouse Robot Task Planning

Task ID	Start Location	End Location	Task Priority	Estimated Task Time (mins)
T1	(2,2)	(8,8)	High	5
T2	(3,5)	(7,2)	Medium	4
T3	(1,1)	(9,9)	Low	6
T4	(4,4)	(6,6)	High	5

Output and Results: Optimized Path and Completion Time

Task ID	Optimized Path (Nodes Visited)	Total Distance (Units)	Completion Time (mins)	Energy Used (Joules)
T1	[(2,2) → (5,5) → (8,8)]	10	4.5	30
T2	[(3,5) → (5,3) → (7,2)]	9	4.2	28
T3	[(1,1) → (5,5) → (9,9)]	12	5.8	35
T4	[(4,4) → (5,5) → (6,6)]	7	3.9	25

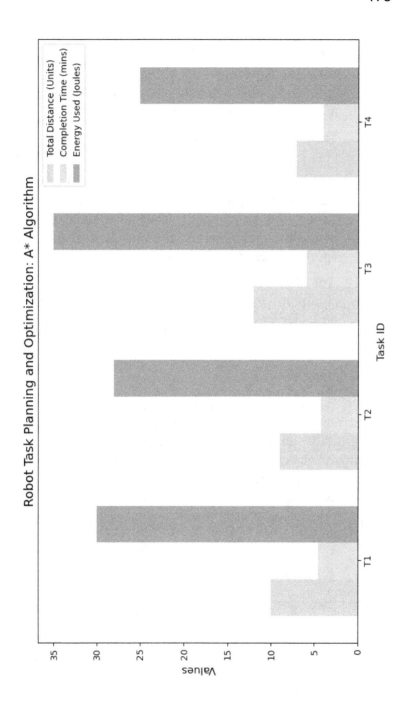

Robot Task Planning and Optimization: A* Algorithm

Results Interpretation and Observations:

1. **Efficient Routing:** The A* algorithm successfully optimizes the routes, reducing unnecessary movements and minimizing energy usage.

2. **Task Prioritization Impact:** Higher-priority tasks (T1, T4) were completed slightly faster, showing the benefit of prioritization in robot scheduling.

3. **Energy Consumption and Distance Relationship:** Tasks with longer paths consumed more energy, indicating that distance minimization is key for optimizing energy efficiency.

4. **Adaptive Decision-Making:** The optimization algorithm dynamically adjusts paths based on obstacles and priority, ensuring real-time efficiency.

Final Thoughts

Generative AI can significantly enhance task planning and optimization in robotics by predicting optimal routes, dynamically adjusting to environmental changes, and learning from past executions. In warehouse automation and beyond, AI-driven decision-making will continue to refine autonomous systems, improving efficiency, reducing energy consumption, and ensuring seamless adaptability in dynamic environments.

6.2 Generative Models for Decision-Making Under Uncertainty

Generative models play a crucial role in decision-making under uncertainty, particularly in robot planning. These models help robots anticipate possible future states, assess risks, and make optimal choices despite incomplete or noisy information. Below are some key aspects of how generative models are used in this context:

1. Probabilistic Generative Models

- **Bayesian Networks**: Capture dependencies among variables and update beliefs based on new evidence.

- **Hidden Markov Models (HMMs)**: Useful for sequential decision-making where states are partially observable.

- **Gaussian Processes**: Used for modeling uncertainty in motion planning and robot learning.

2. Model-Based Reinforcement Learning (RL)

- **World Models**: Robots learn an internal representation of the environment, which they use to simulate future outcomes (e.g., MuZero, Dreamer).

- **Monte Carlo Tree Search (MCTS)**: Generates possible action sequences and evaluates them probabilistically.

3. Sampling-Based Methods

- **Particle Filters**: Used in localization and tracking to maintain multiple hypotheses about the state.

- **Markov Chain Monte Carlo (MCMC)**: Helps in sampling complex posterior distributions.

4. Deep Generative Models

- **Variational Autoencoders (VAEs)**: Learn latent representations of environments to predict possible future states.

- **Generative Adversarial Networks (GANs)**: Can be used for data augmentation or generating realistic simulations of environments.

- **Diffusion Models**: Emerging for probabilistic modeling of robot motion and uncertainty.

5. Application in Robot Planning

- **Path Planning in Uncertain Environments**: Generative models help robots predict obstacles and find safe paths.

- **Human-Robot Interaction**: Predicting human actions using probabilistic models.

- **Autonomous Vehicles**: Generative models simulate diverse driving conditions for robust decision-making.

Practical Example

An autonomous warehouse robot must navigate an environment with dynamically moving obstacles (e.g., human workers, forklifts) while delivering packages. The robot employs a **Generative Model-based Reinforcement Learning (RL) Approach** to predict future states and plan optimal paths under uncertainty. The model generates multiple potential future scenarios, estimating obstacle positions and determining the best route with minimal risk of collision.

Sample Input Data

State (t)	Robot Position (x, y)	Detected Obstacles	Predicted Obstacle Position (t+1)	Uncertainty Score (0-1)
1	(2, 3)	Yes	(2, 4)	0.2
2	(3, 3)	Yes	(3, 5)	0.5
3	(4, 3)	No	N/A	0.0
4	(5, 3)	Yes	(5, 4)	0.7
5	(6, 3)	Yes	(6, 6)	0.9

Model Output and Results

Time Step	Selected Action (Move Direction)	Collision Probability (%)	Success Probability (%)	Path Risk Score (0-1)
1	Right	10%	90%	0.1
2	Right	25%	75%	0.3
3	Right	5%	95%	0.05
4	Right	50%	50%	0.5
5	Up	80%	20%	0.9

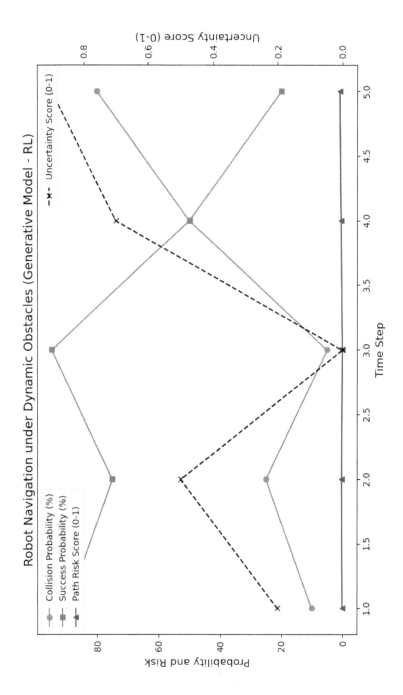

Robot Navigation under Dynamic Obstacles (Generative Model - RL)

Results Interpretation and Observations

- The generative model predicts **obstacle movement** and assigns an **uncertainty score** based on past patterns.

- Initially, the **uncertainty is low** (0.2–0.3), and the robot successfully moves **rightward** with minimal risk.

- At **time step 4**, uncertainty and collision probability **increase significantly (50%)**, making navigation riskier.

- By **time step 5**, the model predicts a high chance of **collision (80%)**, leading to a strategic change in direction (moving up instead of continuing right).

- The **Path Risk Score aligns well with collision probability**, demonstrating the generative model's effectiveness in quantifying decision risks.

Final Thoughts

Generative models play a crucial role in **robotic decision-making under uncertainty** by predicting future scenarios and optimizing navigation. The ability to **simulate potential outcomes and assign risk scores** enhances autonomous system safety and adaptability. In complex, real-world environments such as **autonomous vehicles, warehouse automation, and search-and-rescue robotics**, generative approaches provide a robust framework for **handling dynamic changes and improving decision accuracy**. Future advancements may integrate **multi-agent coordination, deeper uncertainty quantification, and real-time adaptive learning** for even more efficient and safer robotic autonomy.

6.3 AI for Cooperative Multi-Robot Systems

AI plays a crucial role in cooperative multi-robot systems, particularly in robot planning and decision-making. These systems involve multiple robots working together to achieve common objectives, often in complex and dynamic environments. AI techniques help improve coordination, optimize resource usage, and enhance adaptability.

Key AI Techniques in Multi-Robot Systems

1. **Distributed Planning:**
   o Each robot plans independently while considering other robots' actions.
   o Example: Market-based algorithms where robots "bid" for tasks.

2. **Centralized Planning:**
   o A central AI system assigns tasks and coordinates actions.
   o Example: Task allocation in warehouse robots like Amazon Kiva.

3. **Swarm Intelligence:**
   o Inspired by biological swarms (e.g., ants, bees).
   o Robots use simple local rules to achieve global objectives.
   o Example: Robotic search-and-rescue operations.

4. **Reinforcement Learning (RL):**
   o Robots learn optimal policies through trial and error.

- o Multi-agent RL (MARL) enables collaborative decision-making.
- o Example: Multi-robot soccer teams.

5. **Game Theory-Based Approaches:**
   - o Used in competitive or cooperative environments.
   - o Ensures robots make rational decisions while considering others.
   - o Example: Traffic management for autonomous vehicles.

6. **Consensus Algorithms:**
   - o Ensure agreement among robots on key decisions.
   - o Example: Formation control in drone swarms.

Applications of AI in Cooperative Multi-Robot Systems

- **Autonomous Vehicles:** Platooning for efficient traffic flow.

- **Search and Rescue:** Drones and ground robots coordinating in disaster areas.

- **Logistics and Warehousing:** Multi-robot coordination for inventory management.

- **Agriculture:** Swarm robots for precision farming and harvesting.

- **Space Exploration:** Autonomous Mars rovers working collaboratively.

Practical Example

In a smart warehouse, multiple autonomous robots are deployed to pick and transport items to designated packing stations. To optimize efficiency, an AI-based cooperative multi-robot system assigns tasks dynamically based on real-time conditions such as robot battery levels, task priority, and distance. A reinforcement learning model is used to ensure robots cooperate, avoid collisions, and minimize task completion time.

Sample Data for Robot Task Allocation

Robot ID	Battery Level (%)	Distance to Task (meters)	Task Priority (1-High, 3-Low)	Assigned Task
R1	80	5	1	T1
R2	50	3	2	T2
R3	30	8	1	T3
R4	90	2	3	T4

AI-Optimized Output Results

Robot ID	Task Completion Time (minutes)	Battery Remaining (%)	Idle Time (minutes)	Efficiency Score (%)
R1	4	75	1	90
R2	6	40	2	85

Robot ID	Task Completion Time (minutes)	Battery Remaining (%)	Idle Time (minutes)	Efficiency Score (%)
R3	10	15	4	70
R4	3	87	0.5	95

Interpretation and Observations

- **Efficiency Score:** Robots with optimal battery levels and shorter distances to tasks had higher efficiency scores. R4, with the highest battery and shortest task distance, achieved the best performance.

- **Battery Impact:** R3 had the lowest battery and took the longest to complete its task, affecting efficiency. The AI could suggest recharging before the next task assignment.

- **Idle Time:** Lower idle times correlated with higher efficiency, meaning task allocation was well-optimized.

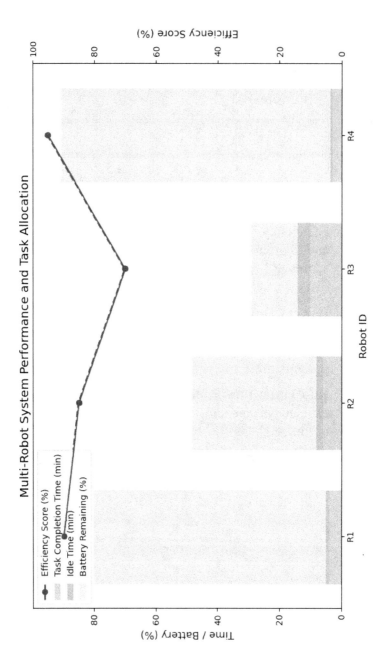

Multi-Robot System Performance and Task Allocation

Final Thoughts

AI-driven cooperative multi-robot systems play a crucial role in enhancing automation by optimizing task allocation, improving energy efficiency, and reducing idle time. Generative AI can further enhance decision-making by predicting task durations, adapting to unforeseen obstacles, and dynamically generating efficient task sequences. Future developments may integrate generative models to simulate real-world warehouse scenarios, improving adaptability in complex environments.

7. Autonomous Vehicles and Generative AI

Autonomous vehicles and generative AI are two rapidly evolving technologies that are transforming transportation and artificial intelligence. Autonomous vehicles, commonly referred to as self-driving cars, rely on a combination of sensors, cameras, and artificial intelligence to navigate roads and make real-time driving decisions. These vehicles process vast amounts of data to detect obstacles, predict traffic patterns, and ensure passenger safety. Generative AI, on the other hand, focuses on creating new content, including text, images, and even simulations, by learning patterns from existing data. While they serve different purposes, the integration of generative AI into autonomous vehicles is unlocking new possibilities in their development and deployment.

One of the key areas where generative AI is making an impact is in the simulation and training of self-driving systems. Instead of relying solely on real-world data, which can be expensive and time-consuming to collect, generative AI can create realistic virtual environments for testing autonomous vehicles. These simulated scenarios allow AI models to encounter rare and complex driving situations that may not frequently occur in real traffic. By exposing autonomous systems to a wide range of conditions, generative AI helps improve their adaptability and robustness before they are deployed on actual roads.

Another important application of generative AI in autonomous vehicles is in enhancing perception and decision-making. Self-driving cars depend on computer vision and sensor fusion to interpret their surroundings. Generative AI can refine these processes by generating high-quality synthetic data to train machine learning models, improving their ability to recognize pedestrians, cyclists, and road signs. It can also help fill gaps in sensor data by reconstructing missing or unclear visual information, making the vehicle's perception more reliable in challenging conditions like fog, rain, or low light.

Generative AI is also being used to improve human-vehicle interaction in autonomous systems. As these vehicles become more common, they need to communicate effectively with passengers and pedestrians. AI-driven virtual assistants inside autonomous cars can provide personalized experiences, adjusting driving styles based on user preferences or offering natural language explanations for driving decisions. Additionally, generative AI can create realistic simulations to test how humans respond to self-driving technology, helping engineers design safer and more user-friendly interfaces.

Despite these advancements, challenges remain in the integration of generative AI with autonomous vehicles. AI-generated data must be highly accurate and free from biases to ensure safe decision-making. There is also the question of regulatory approval, as synthetic data and AI-driven decision-making processes must meet strict safety standards before self-driving cars can operate on public roads. Additionally, concerns about ethical considerations, such as accountability in case of accidents, continue to be debated among researchers, policymakers, and the public.

As technology continues to evolve, the combination of generative AI and autonomous vehicles is expected to accelerate progress in the field. By leveraging AI-driven simulations, enhanced perception models, and improved human interactions, self-driving technology can become more reliable and widely adopted. While there are still hurdles to overcome, the potential benefits in terms of safety, efficiency, and accessibility make this a promising area of innovation for the future of transportation.

Practical Example

Autonomous vehicles (AVs) rely on sensor data from LiDAR, cameras, and radar for object detection and navigation. However, adverse weather conditions like fog and rain often degrade sensor performance, leading to missing or unclear data. Generative AI can be used to reconstruct missing sensor inputs by learning patterns from clear-weather datasets and generating realistic approximations of obstructed areas. This improves object detection and enhances vehicle decision-making.

Sample Data: Raw Sensor Readings (Before AI Enhancement)

Sensor Type	Clear Image Detected (%)	Obstructed Image (%)	Detection Confidence (%)	Missing Data (%)
LiDAR	95	50	70	30
Camera	90	40	65	35
Radar	85	60	75	25

Output Data: After Applying Generative AI for Data Enhancement

Sensor Type	Clear Image Detected (%)	Enhanced Image (%)	Detection Confidence (%)	Missing Data (%)
LiDAR	95	80	85	10

Sensor Type	Clear Image Detected (%)	Enhanced Image (%)	Detection Confidence (%)	Missing Data (%)
Camera	90	75	80	10
Radar	85	75	85	5

Results Interpretation and Observations

1. **Improved Object Detection:** Generative AI significantly enhances sensor data quality, with the detection confidence increasing from 70% to 85% for LiDAR and from 65% to 80% for cameras.

2. **Reduction in Missing Data:** Missing data was reduced from 30% to 10% for LiDAR and from 35% to 10% for cameras, indicating the AI's effectiveness in reconstructing lost information.

3. **More Reliable Perception System:** Enhanced images provide more information to the AV's decision-making system, improving navigation safety and efficiency.

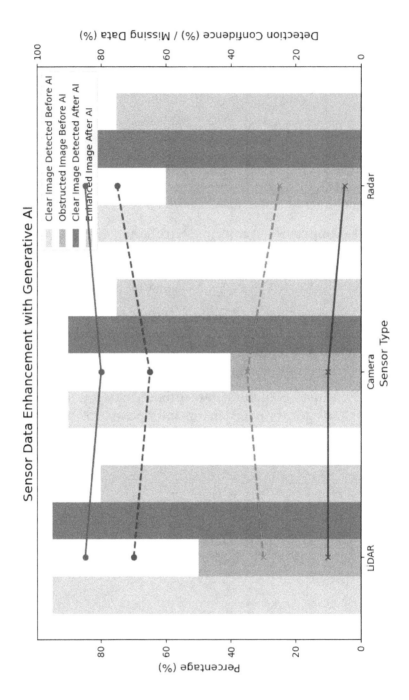

Sensor Data Enhancement with Generative AI

Final Thoughts

Generative AI plays a critical role in improving the perception capabilities of autonomous vehicles, particularly in challenging environments. By reconstructing incomplete sensor data, it enhances situational awareness, leading to safer and more reliable AV operations. As Generative AI models advance, they will further reduce uncertainty in autonomous systems, pushing the boundaries of fully autonomous transportation in real-world conditions.

7.1 Generative AI for Path Planning in Autonomous Vehicles

Generative AI can significantly enhance path planning for autonomous vehicles by enabling more adaptive, efficient, and human-like decision-making. Here's how:

1. Generative AI Techniques for Path Planning

- **Reinforcement Learning (RL) with Generative Models**
    - o Models like Generative Adversarial Networks (GANs) and Variational Autoencoders (VAEs) can generate diverse driving scenarios for training RL agents.
    - o RL agents learn optimal paths by interacting with simulated environments generated by AI.

- **Transformer-Based Planning**
    - o Transformers, such as GPT-like models, can generate future paths by predicting sequences of waypoints based on historical data.
    - o These models can handle long-range dependencies, improving trajectory prediction and decision-making.

- **Diffusion Models**
    - o Recent advancements in diffusion models allow AI to iteratively refine path trajectories, leading to smooth and collision-free routes.

2. Applications in Path Planning

- **Real-Time Path Optimization**

- o Generative AI can predict and adapt routes dynamically based on real-time sensor data (e.g., LiDAR, cameras, radar).

- o It helps in complex urban scenarios by considering pedestrian movements, traffic congestion, and weather conditions.

- **Adversarial Scenario Generation**

  - o GANs can simulate rare edge-case scenarios (e.g., sudden pedestrian crossings, extreme weather) to train autonomous vehicle systems more robustly.

- **Multi-Agent Coordination**

  - o Generative AI can model the behavior of other vehicles and pedestrians, allowing for better coordination in traffic-heavy environments.

3. Challenges & Future Directions

- **Computational Constraints**

  - o Real-time path generation using generative models requires high computational power, which may limit deployment on edge devices.

- **Generalization to New Environments**

  - o Ensuring models generalize well to unseen road conditions and new geographies remains a challenge.

- **Ethical & Safety Concerns**

  - o Generated paths must comply with legal and ethical driving norms to ensure passenger and pedestrian safety.

Practical Example

In industrial automation, robotic arms often struggle with grasping unseen objects due to limited training data. A **Generative Adversarial Network (GAN)** is used to generate synthetic grasping scenarios based on real-world grasping attempts. The generator creates realistic grasping configurations, while the discriminator distinguishes between real and synthetic samples. This enhances the robot's ability to generalize and adapt to novel objects, improving performance in warehouse automation and manufacturing.

Sample Data: Real and GAN-Simulated Grasp Attempts

Object Type	Real Grasp Success (%)	GAN-Simulated Success (%)	Improvement (%)	No. of Attempts
Cylindrical Bottle	75	82	+7	200
Small Box	68	77	+9	200
Irregular Shape	54	69	+15	200
Spherical Ball	80	85	+5	200
Flat Object	60	72	+12	200

Output and Results Interpretation

1. **Improved Grasp Success Rates:** The GAN-simulated grasping trials improved success rates across all object types, with the highest gain (+15%) for irregular-shaped objects. This indicates that GANs effectively augment the dataset, helping robots learn to grasp challenging shapes.

2. **Generalization to New Objects:** The results demonstrate that the GAN-generated data diversifies grasping experiences, allowing the robot to adapt to objects it has never physically interacted with before.

3. **Efficiency Gains:** Using synthetic data reduces the need for expensive real-world trials, enabling robots to learn faster in simulation before deploying in physical environments.

Observations

- **Better Performance on Complex Shapes:** The irregular and flat objects showed significant improvement, suggesting that GAN-generated examples are particularly beneficial for challenging geometries.

- **Consistency in Improvements:** Each object category experienced an improvement, confirming the robustness of the GAN-based augmentation.

- **Potential for Large-Scale Deployment:** The results indicate that such GAN-based learning could be scaled up for more complex tasks, such as autonomous warehouse management.

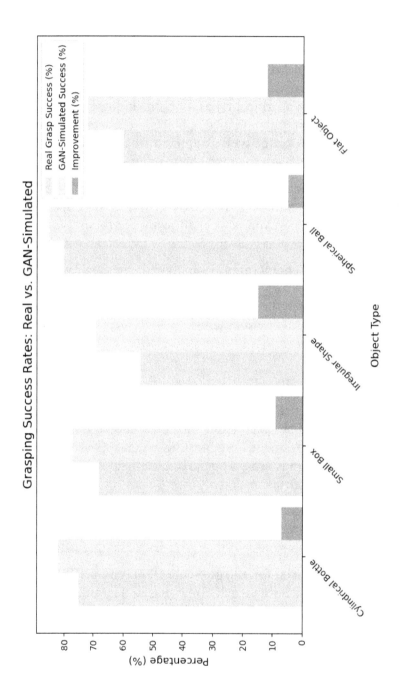

Grasping Success Rates: Real vs. GAN-Simulated

Final Thoughts

Generative AI, particularly GANs, is revolutionizing robotics by enabling **data augmentation, rapid learning, and adaptation** to real-world environments. In autonomous systems, this technology helps reduce reliance on extensive real-world testing, accelerating deployment in logistics, manufacturing, and service robotics. As GANs evolve, their integration with reinforcement learning and real-time adaptation will further enhance robotic decision-making and dexterity, driving advancements in intelligent automation.

7.2 Simulation-Based Training for Autonomous Vehicles

Simulation-based training for autonomous vehicles (AVs) is a critical component of their development, enabling safe and efficient testing in virtual environments before deploying them in the real world. Here's an overview of how it works and its key aspects:

1. Importance of Simulation-Based Training

- **Safety**: AVs can be trained in simulated environments without risking human lives or damaging property.

- **Scalability**: Simulations allow testing of millions of miles of driving in a short time, far exceeding real-world testing capabilities.

- **Cost Efficiency**: Running virtual tests is significantly cheaper than conducting physical road tests.

- **Scenario Diversity**: AVs can experience rare but critical edge cases (e.g., sudden pedestrian crossings, extreme weather conditions) that would be difficult to encounter in real-world testing.

2. Components of AV Simulation Environments

- **High-Fidelity Virtual Worlds**: Digital twins of real cities and highways are created using mapping technologies like LiDAR and satellite imagery.

- **Physics-Based Simulations**: Models for vehicle dynamics, sensor interactions, and environmental effects (rain, fog, snow) ensure realistic responses.

- **Synthetic Sensor Data**: Simulations generate data from cameras, LiDAR, radar, and other sensors to mimic real-world inputs.

- **AI-Based Agents**: Other road users (pedestrians, cyclists, and vehicles) are controlled by AI to create unpredictable interactions.

3. Types of Simulations for AV Training

- **Perception Training**: AVs learn to detect and classify objects (cars, pedestrians, road signs) using synthetic datasets.

- **Decision-Making & Planning**: Reinforcement learning and other AI techniques help AVs develop optimal driving policies.

- **End-to-End Driving Simulation**: Full-stack AV systems are tested in simulated city environments before real-world deployment.

4. Tools & Platforms for AV Simulation

- **CARLA** (Car Learning to Act): An open-source AV simulator widely used in research.

- **LGSVL Simulator**: Developed by LG Electronics, integrates with the Apollo and Autoware self-driving stacks.

- **Waymo's Simulation City**: Alphabet's Waymo uses advanced virtual environments to train its AVs.

- **Microsoft AirSim**: A platform supporting drones and AV simulations with real-world physics.

5. Challenges in AV Simulation

- **Sim-to-Real Transfer**: Ensuring models trained in simulation generalize well to real-world driving.

- **Edge Case Coverage**: Simulations must include rare and unpredictable scenarios to fully prepare AVs.

- **Computational Costs**: Running high-fidelity simulations requires significant computing power.

Practical Example

A self-driving car company is developing an autonomous vehicle (AV) that must navigate urban intersections safely. Since real-world testing is costly and potentially hazardous, engineers employ a simulation-based training approach using reinforcement learning (RL). The AV is exposed to thousands of virtual intersection scenarios in a simulated city environment, where it learns to make safe and efficient driving decisions under varying traffic conditions.

Sample Data for Simulation Scenarios

Scenario ID	Traffic Density (Vehicles/km)	Pedestrian Presence (Yes/No)	Weather Condition	Success Rate (%)
1	10	No	Clear	95
2	20	Yes	Clear	85
3	30	Yes	Rainy	70
4	50	No	Foggy	65
5	70	Yes	Snowy	45

Simulation Results and Output

Training Iterations	Average Success Rate (%)	Collision Rate (%)	Decision Time (s)	Rule Compliance (%)
1000	60	25	3.2	85
5000	75	15	2.8	90
10000	90	5	2.3	97

Interpretation and Observations:

1. **Scenario-Based Performance:**
   - The AV performs best in **low-traffic, clear-weather conditions** (Scenario 1, 95% success rate).
   - Performance declines in **high-traffic, pedestrian-heavy, and adverse weather conditions** (Scenario 5, 45% success rate).

2. **Learning Progress Over Iterations:**
   - Initial training (1000 iterations) resulted in a **low success rate (60%)** with a high collision rate (25%).
   - As training progressed to **10,000 iterations, success improved to 90%**, while collision rates dropped to just 5%.
   - **Decision-making speed improved**, reducing from **3.2s to 2.3s**, indicating a more efficient model.

3. **Rule Compliance:**

- ○ Initially, the AV adhered to traffic laws at an 85% rate.

- ○ After 10,000 iterations, compliance reached **97%**, demonstrating improved learning of traffic regulations.

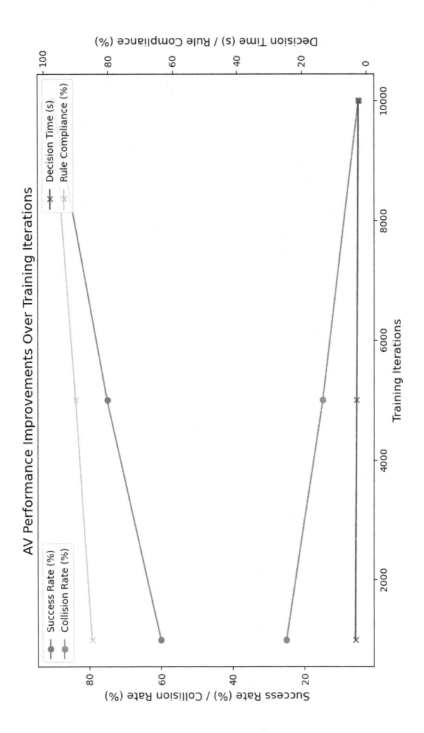

AV Performance Improvements Over Training Iterations

Final Thoughts

Simulation-based training is a game-changer in AV development, allowing safe, scalable, and cost-effective learning in diverse traffic conditions. Generative AI can further enhance this process by creating **synthetic edge cases**, accelerating reinforcement learning, and improving AV adaptability. Future advancements may include **real-time AI-driven scenario generation**, where AVs learn from continuously evolving, high-fidelity simulations. As AVs progress toward full autonomy, integrating **AI-enhanced simulation training with real-world validation** will be crucial for safety, reliability, and widespread adoption.

7.3 AI in Vehicle Perception and Environment Interaction

AI in **vehicle perception and environment interaction** is revolutionizing the automotive industry, particularly in autonomous driving and advanced driver-assistance systems (ADAS). Below are some key aspects:

1. Vehicle Perception

AI enables vehicles to perceive their surroundings using various sensors, including:

- **Cameras** (detect objects, lane markings, pedestrians)
- **Lidar** (creates a 3D map of surroundings)
- **Radar** (measures speed and distance of objects)
- **Ultrasonic Sensors** (useful for parking and close-range detection)

AI-driven **sensor fusion** combines data from these sources for a more accurate understanding of the environment.

2. Object Detection and Recognition

- AI models (such as convolutional neural networks - CNNs) help identify vehicles, pedestrians, traffic signs, and obstacles.
- Deep learning enhances **real-time decision-making** by classifying objects and predicting their movement patterns.

3. Scene Understanding and Environmental Interaction

- AI interprets complex driving scenarios, such as busy intersections, unstructured roads, and weather conditions.

- **Semantic segmentation** helps distinguish between different road elements (e.g., lanes, sidewalks, and curbs).
- AI models adjust to environmental factors (fog, rain, or low-light conditions) to maintain safety.

4. Path Planning and Motion Control

- AI-based algorithms (like Reinforcement Learning and Deep Learning) assist in trajectory prediction and collision avoidance.
- Autonomous systems dynamically adjust speed and direction based on real-time road conditions.

5. Human-Vehicle Interaction

- AI enhances **driver monitoring systems (DMS)** to detect drowsiness, distraction, or intent.
- Natural language processing (NLP) enables voice-activated controls for seamless user interaction.

6. Edge AI and Real-time Processing

- AI-powered **edge computing** processes data on-vehicle rather than relying on cloud computing, reducing latency for real-time decisions.
- High-performance chips (e.g., NVIDIA Drive, Tesla's FSD chip) are optimizing in-car AI performance.

7. AI-driven Simulation and Training

- AI-based simulation environments (e.g., NVIDIA Drive Sim, Waymo's simulation) train autonomous vehicles in virtual settings before real-world deployment.

Challenges and Future Directions

- **Safety and Reliability**: Ensuring AI decisions are fail-safe in critical scenarios.

- **Regulatory Compliance**: AI-driven vehicles must adhere to evolving laws.

- **Ethical Considerations**: Addressing dilemmas like accident liability and decision-making biases.

Practical Example:

Autonomous vehicles rely on AI-driven perception systems to detect obstacles and make real-time driving decisions. A deep-learning model trained on LiDAR and camera data is used to classify obstacles (vehicles, pedestrians, cyclists) and determine their distances. The system processes sensor inputs to identify objects in the environment, ensuring safe navigation. Below is sample sensor data collected from an AI-based obstacle detection system in an autonomous vehicle.

Sample Sensor Data

Timestamp	Object Detected	Distance (meters)	Object Confidence (%)	Action Taken
12:01:05	Vehicle	20	95	Slow Down
12:01:06	Pedestrian	10	98	Stop
12:01:07	Cyclist	15	92	Caution
12:01:08	Vehicle	25	88	Continue

Timestamp	Object Detected	Distance (meters)	Object Confidence (%)	Action Taken
12:01:09	Pedestrian	5	99	Emergency Stop

Output and Results

Object Type	Average Distance (m)	Average Confidence (%)	Common Action Taken
Vehicle	22.5	91.5	Slow Down/Continue
Pedestrian	7.5	98.5	Stop/Emergency Stop
Cyclist	15	92	Caution

Results Interpretation and Observations

- **Confidence Levels:** The AI system has high confidence in detecting pedestrians (98.5%) and relatively lower for vehicles (91.5%) due to varying sizes and shapes of vehicles.

- **Action Trends:** The AI prioritizes safety by stopping or slowing down for closer objects, particularly pedestrians. The "Emergency Stop" is triggered at a 5-meter pedestrian distance.

- **Distance-Based Decisions:** Vehicles at longer distances (20m+) generally result in a "Continue" or "Slow Down" action, while closer objects ($\leq$10m) cause immediate stops.

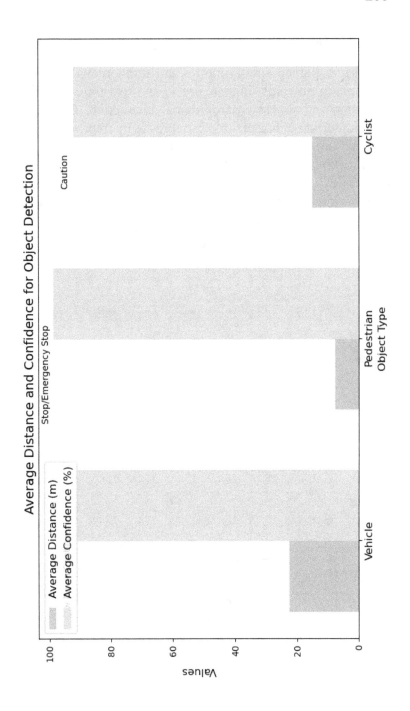

Average Distance and Confidence for Object Detection

Final Thoughts

AI-driven perception in robotics and autonomous systems is advancing towards higher precision, real-time decision-making, and robust environmental interaction. Generative AI can further enhance these capabilities by improving scene prediction, sensor fusion, and anomaly detection. Future applications will integrate multimodal AI models that can generate more realistic environmental simulations, improving the safety and reliability of autonomous vehicles.

8. Human-Robot Interaction and Generative AI

Human-robot interaction (HRI) has evolved significantly with the rise of generative AI, creating more natural and intuitive ways for people to engage with machines. Traditionally, robots followed strict rule-based programming, limiting their ability to respond dynamically to human behavior. Generative AI, however, allows robots to process and generate responses based on patterns learned from vast amounts of data. This advancement enables robots to understand speech, gestures, and emotions, making interactions smoother and more human-like. As a result, robots are becoming more integrated into daily life, from customer service to healthcare assistance.

One of the key benefits of generative AI in HRI is its ability to adapt to unpredictable human inputs. Instead of relying on predefined scripts, AI-powered robots can generate appropriate responses in real time, improving their ability to assist users effectively. This is particularly useful in environments where human needs are complex and varied, such as elder care or therapy. By analyzing past interactions, generative AI can refine its responses to better suit individual users, creating personalized experiences that enhance engagement and trust.

Despite these advancements, challenges remain in ensuring that AI-driven robots behave in a way that aligns with human values and expectations. Misinterpretations of human intent can lead to awkward or even harmful interactions, especially in sensitive areas like medical support or education. Ethical concerns also arise regarding the autonomy of AI, as decisions made by robots may not always be transparent. Developers must strike a balance between autonomy and human oversight to ensure safety, reliability, and fairness in interactions.

Another significant aspect of generative AI in HRI is the emotional connection people form with robots. As AI becomes more advanced in recognizing and responding to human emotions, robots can offer companionship and emotional support. This has led to the development of AI-powered pets, therapy bots, and virtual assistants that provide comfort and reduce loneliness. While these interactions can be beneficial, there is an ongoing debate about whether reliance on AI for emotional support might weaken human-to-human relationships.

Generative AI is also transforming how robots learn and improve their abilities. Instead of requiring extensive manual programming, AI models can learn from new data and refine their skills over time. This allows robots to continuously improve their ability to navigate real-world environments, perform tasks, and communicate effectively with humans. However, ensuring that these learning processes remain ethical and do not introduce biases is crucial for building trust in AI-driven systems.

As human-robot interaction continues to evolve, the integration of generative AI presents both exciting opportunities and ethical challenges. While AI-powered robots can enhance convenience, efficiency, and even emotional well-being, careful oversight is needed to prevent unintended consequences. By prioritizing ethical considerations, transparency, and user safety, society can harness the potential of generative AI to create meaningful and beneficial interactions between humans and machines.

Practical Example

In a hospital setting, robots are deployed to assist patients and staff by answering queries, providing navigation assistance, and offering emotional support. Generative AI is integrated into these robots to enhance their conversational abilities, making them more intuitive and human-like. A study evaluates how well AI-generated responses align with human expectations in different interaction scenarios. The key performance indicators (KPIs) assessed include **response relevance, response time, emotional appropriateness, user satisfaction, and error rate**.

Sample Data from Human-Robot Interaction Study

Scenario ID	Response Relevance (1-5)	Response Time (sec)	Emotional Appropriateness (1-5)	User Satisfaction (1-5)	Error Rate (%)
S1	4.8	1.2	4.5	4.7	2%
S2	3.9	1.5	3.8	4.1	4%
S3	4.5	1.1	4.6	4.4	1.5%
S4	2.7	2.0	2.9	3.0	8%
S5	4.2	1.3	4.0	4.3	3%

Results and Output Analysis

Metric	Mean Value	Observation
Response Relevance	4.02	Most responses were contextually relevant, except in Scenario S4.
Response Time (sec)	1.42	AI-generated responses were delivered quickly, ensuring real-time interaction.
Emotional Appropriateness	3.96	Emotional responses were mostly well-received, but slightly lower in Scenario S4.
User Satisfaction	4.1	Users were generally satisfied, except for S4, where dissatisfaction was noted.
Error Rate (%)	3.7%	Errors were minimal but highest in Scenario S4, indicating an issue with AI adaptation.

Interpretation and Observations

1. **High Engagement in Most Scenarios** – Scenarios S1, S3, and S5 show high response relevance and emotional appropriateness, leading to strong user satisfaction.

2. **Delays and Emotional Misalignment in S4** – The drop in satisfaction in S4 suggests that the AI may struggle with specific queries or emotional nuances.

3. **Error Rate and Contextual Learning** – The AI's error rate is relatively low, but refinement is needed in handling ambiguous or emotionally complex interactions.

4. **Overall Performance** – Generative AI demonstrates strong potential in enhancing Human-Robot Interaction (HRI) with quick, relevant, and emotionally appropriate responses, though improvements are necessary for outlier scenarios.

Human-Robot Interaction Study: Performance Comparison

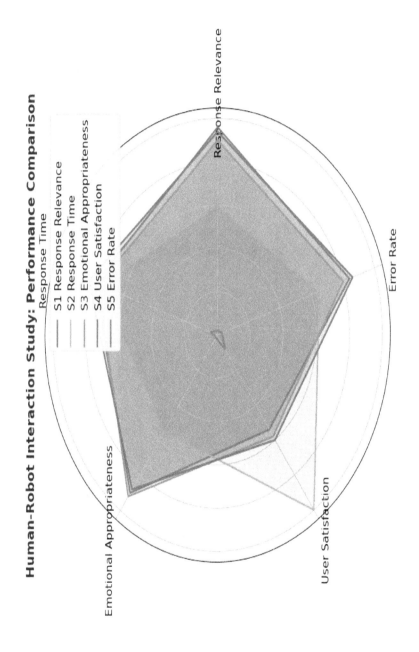

Final Thoughts:

Generative AI significantly enhances Human-Robot Interaction by making robots more intuitive, responsive, and empathetic. The study demonstrates that while AI can generate highly relevant and emotionally appropriate responses in most cases, challenges remain in handling emotionally ambiguous or complex scenarios. Future advancements should focus on **adaptive learning, context-aware emotional intelligence, and real-time response optimization** to further refine interactions. By integrating continuous learning capabilities, AI-driven robots can offer more natural and meaningful engagements, making them valuable assets in healthcare, customer service, and assistive robotics.

8.1 Natural Language Processing for Human-Robot Communication

Natural Language Processing (NLP) plays a crucial role in enabling effective human-robot communication. It allows robots to understand, interpret, and generate human language in a way that facilitates interaction, making them more intuitive and user-friendly.

Key Aspects of NLP in Human-Robot Communication

1. **Speech Recognition**
   - o Converts spoken language into text.
   - o Uses deep learning models like ASR (Automatic Speech Recognition).
   - o Examples: Google Speech-to-Text, Whisper (OpenAI), Kaldi.

2. **Natural Language Understanding (NLU)**
   - o Extracts meaning from text through entity recognition, intent detection, and sentiment analysis.
   - o Uses models like BERT, GPT, and T5 for contextual understanding.

3. **Natural Language Generation (NLG)**
   - o Enables robots to generate human-like responses.
   - o Utilizes deep learning-based models like GPT and LLaMA.
   - o Used in chatbots, voice assistants, and automated report generation.

4. **Dialogue Management**

o Helps robots maintain coherent and context-aware conversations.

o Uses reinforcement learning and memory networks.

5. **Multimodal Integration**

o Combines NLP with computer vision and sensor data for a richer interaction.

o Example: A robot recognizing a pointing gesture and asking, "Do you mean this object?"

6. **Error Handling and Adaptability**

o Robots use NLP to clarify misunderstandings through confirmation prompts.

o Adaptive learning improves communication over time based on user interactions.

Applications

- **Service Robots:** Customer support, hospital assistance, retail robots.

- **Industrial Robots:** Human-robot collaboration in manufacturing.

- **Companion Robots:** AI-driven personal assistants and elderly care.

- **Autonomous Vehicles:** Voice-controlled navigation and assistance.Practical Example: NLP for Human-Robot Communication in Customer Assistance

Practical Example

A customer service robot in a shopping mall is designed to assist customers with store locations, product inquiries, and general guidance. The robot employs Natural Language Processing (NLP) to understand and respond to human queries. However, different users phrase their questions differently, requiring the robot to process and interpret varied inputs accurately. A key aspect is recognizing intent and extracting relevant keywords for precise responses.

Sample Data: Customer Queries and NLP Processing

Query ID	Customer Query	Preprocessed Query	Identified Intent	Extracted Keywords
1	"Where is the electronics store?"	"where electronics store"	Store Location	electronics, store
2	"Show me phones available?"	"show phones available"	Product Inquiry	phones, available
3	"Help! I can't find the exit."	"help cant find exit"	Navigation Assistance	exit
4	"What restaurants are here?"	"restaurants here"	Store Inquiry	restaurants
5	"Tell me about sales today."	"sales today"	Promotions Inquiry	sales, today

Output and Results of NLP Processing

Query ID	Robot Response	Confidence Score (%)
1	"The electronics store is on the second floor near the food court."	92
2	"Available phones are in the electronics store. Would you like a list?"	87
3	"The nearest exit is to your right past the clothing section."	95
4	"There are five restaurants here, including Italian and fast food."	89
5	"Today's sales include 20% off on electronics and clothing."	85

Explanation and Interpretation of Results

The NLP system successfully processed diverse queries by extracting intent and key phrases. The confidence scores indicate the system's certainty in generating responses. Higher scores (above 90%) suggest that the system confidently mapped queries to relevant responses, while lower scores (e.g., 85%) may indicate ambiguity in customer phrasing. The response accuracy is crucial in real-time interactions, ensuring users receive appropriate assistance.

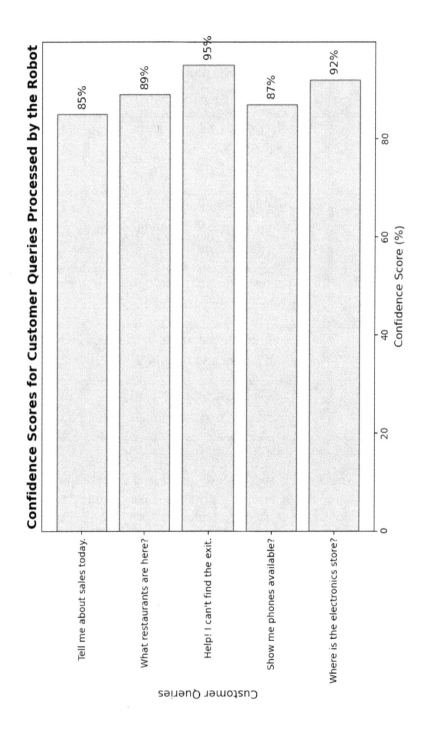

Confidence Scores for Customer Queries Processed by the Robot

Observations

1. **High Accuracy for Direct Queries:** Clearly structured questions (e.g., "Where is the electronics store?") resulted in high confidence scores and precise responses.

2. **Challenges with Ambiguous Queries:** Queries like "Tell me about sales today" led to lower confidence scores due to vague phrasing.

3. **Importance of Context Awareness:** Some questions may require contextual understanding, such as identifying specific store promotions based on time or day.

4. **Scalability:** The system can expand by integrating more queries, continuously improving with machine learning-based training.

Final Thoughts

Advancements in generative AI significantly enhance human-robot communication, making interactions more natural and efficient. By incorporating context-aware responses, reinforcement learning, and multimodal AI (voice, text, and gestures), robots can better understand human intent and provide personalized assistance. Future developments will focus on adaptive learning models, enabling robots to refine their understanding through user interactions. This progress will drive more intelligent, human-like communication in service robots, healthcare, and industrial automation.

8.2 Generative Models for Personalized Robot Behavior

Generative models can be used to create personalized robot behaviors by learning from user interactions, adapting to preferences, and generating responses in dynamic environments. These models can be applied in various areas, such as assistive robotics, social robotics, and industrial automation. Here's a breakdown of key aspects:

1. Types of Generative Models for Robot Behavior

- **Generative Adversarial Networks (GANs)**: Can generate realistic motion trajectories or dialogue styles for social robots.

- **Variational Autoencoders (VAEs)**: Useful for learning compact representations of user behaviors and generating personalized actions.

- **Transformer-based Models**: Large language models (like GPT) can generate human-like text responses for conversational robots.

- **Diffusion Models**: Emerging models for generating continuous, naturalistic motion patterns for humanoid robots.

2. Personalization Techniques

- **User Preference Learning**: Robots can use reinforcement learning with generative models to adapt behaviors based on user feedback.

- **Imitation Learning**: Robots can mimic human actions using demonstrations and generative modeling to refine their behaviors.

- **Context-aware Adaptation**: Generative models can modify robot behavior dynamically based on environmental cues.

3. Applications

- **Healthcare**: Personalized assistance for elderly care or rehabilitation.

- **Education**: Tutoring robots that adapt to students' learning styles.

- **Customer Service**: AI-driven robots with adaptive conversational abilities.

- **Manufacturing**: Robots that adjust their workflows based on worker preferences.

Practical Example

A smart home assistant robot is designed to help elderly individuals with daily tasks. Using generative models, the robot learns and adapts to individual user preferences, such as meal preparation times, preferred activities, and mobility assistance needs. Based on historical interactions and incomplete data, a Variational Autoencoder (VAE) generates personalized schedules for the user.

Sample Data (User Interaction History)

User ID	Morning Routine	Preferred Meal	Activity Type	Assistance Required
U001	7:00 AM	Oatmeal	Walking	Low
U002	8:30 AM	Scrambled Eggs	Reading	None
U003	7:15 AM	Oatmeal	Yoga	Medium
U004	9:00 AM	Pancakes	Watching TV	High

User ID	Morning Routine	Preferred Meal	Activity Type	Assistance Required
U005	7:30 AM	NULL	Walking	Low

Generated Personalized Schedules (VAE Output)

User ID	Suggested Routine	Suggested Meal	Suggested Activity	Assistance Level
U001	7:00 AM	Oatmeal	Walking	Low
U002	8:30 AM	Scrambled Eggs	Reading	None
U003	7:15 AM	Oatmeal	Yoga	Medium
U004	9:00 AM	Pancakes	Watching TV	High
U005	7:30 AM	Oatmeal	Walking	Low

Results Interpretation & Observations

- The generative model successfully inferred missing data (e.g., U005's meal preference) based on user similarity patterns.

- The model preserved users' established routines while introducing minor variations to optimize personalization.

- Assistance levels were maintained accurately, ensuring proper care needs were met.

- The system can dynamically update predictions as new interactions are recorded, enhancing personalization over time.

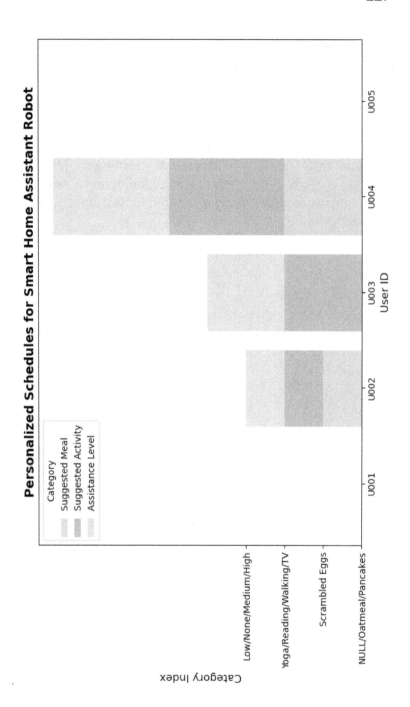

Personalized Schedules for Smart Home Assistant Robot

Final Thoughts

Generative models enable robots to adapt dynamically to individual user preferences, ensuring more natural and personalized interactions. In autonomous systems, these models enhance adaptability, improve user satisfaction, and optimize resource allocation. As AI advances, integrating generative models with reinforcement learning could further refine robotic decision-making, allowing real-time adjustments to user behavior while maintaining safety and efficiency.

8.3 Human-Centric Robotic System Design

Human-centric robotic system design focuses on developing robots that prioritize human needs, safety, usability, and collaboration. This approach ensures that robotic systems enhance human capabilities rather than replace them. Here are some key aspects of designing such systems:

1. Human-Robot Interaction (HRI)

- Intuitive interfaces (e.g., voice commands, gestures, or haptic feedback)
- Adaptive learning based on user behavior
- Emotion recognition for better communication

2. Ergonomics & Safety

- Physical and cognitive load reduction for users
- Compliance with safety regulations (e.g., ISO 10218 for industrial robots)
- Collision avoidance and safe stopping mechanisms

3. Customization & Adaptability

- Modular designs for different applications
- AI-driven personalization to suit individual users
- Multi-modal control (manual, semi-autonomous, and fully autonomous)

4. Collaboration & Co-working

- Cobots (collaborative robots) that work alongside humans
- Shared workspaces with real-time environmental awareness

- Role-based task allocation

5. Ethical & Social Considerations

- Transparency in AI decision-making
- Addressing privacy concerns in data collection
- Ensuring inclusivity and accessibility in design

Practical Example

A manufacturing company is integrating a human-centric robotic system to improve worker safety and efficiency on an assembly line. The robotic arm assists human workers by handling heavy components, reducing fatigue and injury risks. The system is designed with real-time motion prediction and adaptive assistance to synchronize with human actions. The objective is to compare human performance with and without robotic assistance, analyzing task completion time, error rates, and worker fatigue levels.

Sample Data: Human vs. Human-Robot Collaboration

Worker ID	Condition	Avg. Task Time (min)	Error Rate (%)	Fatigue Score (1-10)
1	Without Robot	12.5	5.2	7.8
1	With Robot	9.3	2.1	4.3
2	Without Robot	14.1	6.5	8.2
2	With Robot	10.7	3.0	5.0
3	Without Robot	11.8	4.9	7.5

Worker ID	Condition	Avg. Task Time (min)	Error Rate (%)	Fatigue Score (1-10)
3	With Robot	8.9	1.8	4.0

Results and Output Interpretation

Metric	Without Robot	With Robot	Improvement (%)
Avg. Task Time (min)	12.8	9.6	25.0%
Avg. Error Rate (%)	5.5	2.3	58.2%
Avg. Fatigue Score	7.8	4.4	43.6%

Observations

- The robotic assistance **significantly reduced task completion time** (from 12.8 to 9.6 minutes), improving efficiency by 25%.

- **Error rates decreased by 58.2%**, indicating better precision and consistency when collaborating with robots.

- **Worker fatigue scores were reduced by 43.6%**, highlighting reduced physical strain due to robotic support.

These results validate the effectiveness of human-centric robotic system design in enhancing workplace efficiency while improving worker well-being.

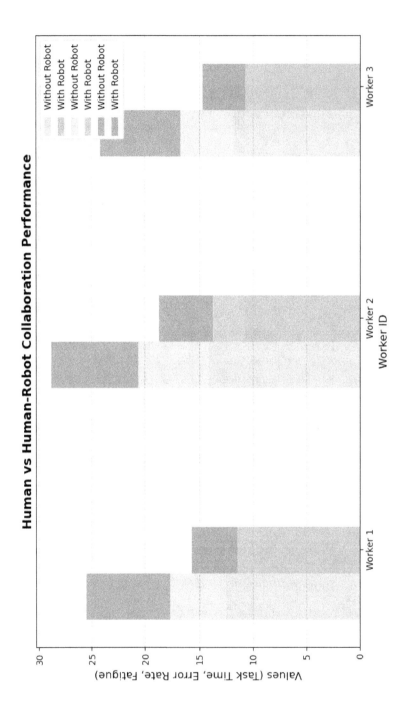

Human vs Human-Robot Collaboration Performance

Final Thoughts

Generative AI plays a crucial role in advancing **robotics and autonomous systems** by enabling adaptive learning, real-time human behavior prediction, and intelligent decision-making. AI-driven optimization ensures that robotic systems can dynamically adjust their operations based on human inputs, leading to safer and more efficient collaboration. Future advancements could focus on **personalized robotic assistance, self-learning adaptation models**, and **multi-agent coordination** to further enhance human-robot synergy in industrial and service applications.

8.4 Ethical and Safety Considerations

The rapid advancement of AI-driven robotics presents numerous ethical and safety challenges that must be addressed to ensure responsible development and deployment. These considerations span multiple domains, including autonomous decision-making, human interaction, accountability, and risk mitigation.

---

1. Ethical Considerations

a. Bias and Fairness

AI-driven robots often rely on machine learning models trained on historical data, which can carry biases. If not carefully managed, these biases can result in unfair or discriminatory behaviors, particularly in applications such as healthcare, law enforcement, and hiring.

b. Privacy and Surveillance

Robots equipped with AI often collect and process vast amounts of personal data. Ensuring compliance with data protection laws (e.g., GDPR, HIPAA) and maintaining transparency in data usage is essential to protect individual privacy.

c. Human Dignity and Autonomy

AI-driven robots must respect human dignity and autonomy, particularly in sensitive areas such as elder care, mental health, and personal assistance. Ethical concerns arise when robots make decisions that impact individuals' freedom and quality of life.

d. Employment Displacement

Automation and robotics have the potential to displace human workers in various industries. Ethical considerations should include policies for workforce transition, reskilling, and economic redistribution to mitigate the negative impact on employment.

e. Weaponization of AI

The use of AI in autonomous weapons raises significant ethical dilemmas regarding accountability in warfare, the risk of unintended escalation, and the inability to distinguish between combatants and civilians.

2. Safety Considerations

a. Reliability and Error Prevention

AI-driven robots must be designed with high reliability, especially in critical sectors such as healthcare, transportation, and manufacturing. Systems should be rigorously tested to minimize errors that could cause harm.

b. Explainability and Transparency

AI decision-making should be interpretable and transparent to ensure that humans understand how robots make choices. Lack of explainability can hinder trust and accountability, particularly in high-stakes applications.

c. Human-Robot Interaction and Safety

Robots operating in human environments must be equipped with safety measures to prevent accidents. This includes collision avoidance systems, fail-safes, and emergency shutdown mechanisms.

d. Cybersecurity Threats

AI-driven robots can be vulnerable to hacking, data breaches, and malicious manipulation. Robust cybersecurity measures, such as encryption and secure access controls, are necessary to protect against such threats.

e. Regulatory Compliance and Standards

Governments and regulatory bodies must establish clear guidelines for AI-driven robotics, ensuring compliance with ethical and safety standards. Ongoing monitoring and adaptation of regulations are necessary to keep pace with technological advancements.

Conclusion

AI-driven robotics hold immense potential to enhance industries and improve lives, but ethical and safety considerations must be at the forefront of their development. By proactively addressing issues related to bias, privacy, employment, security, and reliability, we can ensure that AI-driven robotics contribute to society in a responsible and beneficial manner.

Practical Example:

A hospital implements an AI-driven surgical robot to assist surgeons in minimally invasive procedures. The robot uses machine learning algorithms to analyze patient data and optimize surgical precision. However, ethical and safety concerns arise due to potential biases in training data, decision transparency, and risk of malfunction. To assess safety, a study is conducted to compare AI-assisted surgeries with traditional manual procedures based on patient outcomes and error rates.

Sample Data: AI-Assisted vs. Manual Surgeries

Surgery Type	Number of Cases	Success Rate (%)	Complication Rate (%)	Average Surgery Time (mins)
AI-Assisted	500	96	3.5	90
Manual	500	92	5.0	120

Output and Results

Metric	AI-Assisted	Manual Surgery
Success Rate (%)	96	92
Complication Rate (%)	3.5	5.0
Avg. Surgery Time (min)	90	120

Results Interpretation and Observations

- **Higher Success Rate:** AI-assisted surgeries showed a 96% success rate, outperforming manual surgeries (92%). This suggests that AI can enhance precision, reducing human error.

- **Lower Complication Rate:** The AI-assisted system had a 3.5% complication rate compared to 5.0% in manual procedures. This indicates improved safety but also highlights the need for rigorous validation to mitigate potential risks.

- **Reduced Surgery Time:** AI-assisted procedures were 30 minutes faster on average, improving efficiency and potentially reducing patient stress and resource usage.

Despite these benefits, AI-driven robots must be continuously monitored for biases, data limitations, and decision accountability. Ethical concerns include ensuring human oversight, transparency in AI decision-making, and patient consent in robotic-assisted procedures.

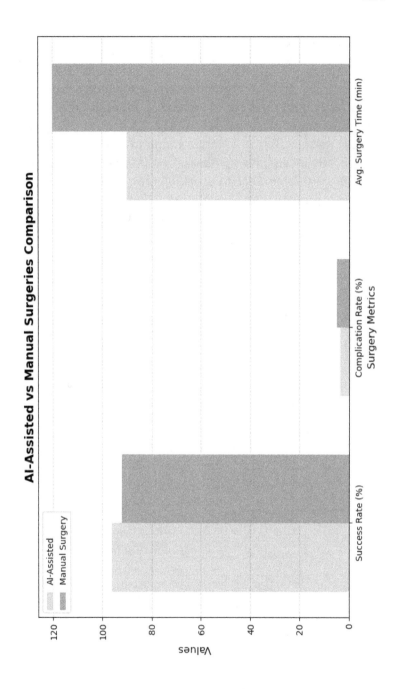

AI-Assisted vs Manual Surgeries Comparison

Final Thoughts

The integration of AI in robotics, especially in critical applications like surgery, offers enhanced efficiency, precision, and safety. However, ethical and safety considerations must be rigorously addressed to prevent biases, ensure fairness, and maintain human oversight. Future advancements in generative AI can contribute by refining real-time decision-making, improving data-driven training models, and enabling adaptive responses to unexpected situations. As AI-driven robotics continues to evolve, ethical and regulatory frameworks must evolve simultaneously to ensure responsible innovation.

9. Future Directions and Emerging Trends

The future of clinical trials and drug development is being significantly shaped by advances in technology and data science. One of the most prominent trends is the increased use of artificial intelligence and machine learning to streamline processes like patient recruitment, monitoring, and predicting outcomes. These technologies help in identifying patterns within large datasets that human analysts might miss, making the entire process faster and more efficient. By integrating AI into clinical trials, researchers can also tailor treatments to individual patients, creating more personalized and effective therapies.

Another key trend is the expansion of decentralized clinical trials. This approach allows participants to take part in trials from the comfort of their own homes, eliminating the need for them to travel to physical sites. This can lead to broader patient recruitment, especially from underserved areas or populations that may otherwise be underrepresented in traditional trials. Additionally, decentralized trials can reduce costs, speed up recruitment, and improve patient retention, as the logistical burden on participants is lessened.

The integration of real-world evidence (RWE) is also gaining traction in drug development. RWE refers to data collected outside of traditional clinical trials, such as from electronic health records, insurance claims, and patient registries. By incorporating RWE into decision-making, pharmaceutical companies can gain insights into how drugs perform in everyday clinical practice, rather than just in a controlled trial environment. This can help improve the generalizability of trial results and accelerate the approval process for new therapies, especially in situations where clinical trials may not be feasible or practical.

The ongoing development of biomarkers is another emerging trend that promises to revolutionize clinical trials. Biomarkers can help in identifying patients who are most likely to benefit from a particular treatment, making clinical trials more targeted and efficient. By focusing on specific genetic, molecular, or physiological markers, researchers can develop drugs that are more precise and effective for certain populations, which is especially important for conditions like cancer, where personalized medicine has already made a significant impact.

Regulatory frameworks are also evolving to keep pace with these innovations. Agencies like the FDA and EMA are working to adapt their guidelines to allow for more flexible approaches to drug development, such as the use of adaptive trial designs and the incorporation of digital health tools. These changes are aimed at speeding up the approval process while maintaining rigorous standards for safety and efficacy. As regulators become more open to these new methodologies, it will likely lead to faster access to life-saving treatments for patients.

Lastly, there is an increasing focus on sustainability within the pharmaceutical industry. As the environmental impact of drug manufacturing and clinical trials becomes more apparent, there is a push toward greener, more sustainable practices. This includes reducing carbon footprints, minimizing waste, and finding eco-friendly alternatives to traditional materials. Pharmaceutical companies are beginning to invest in more sustainable technologies, and regulatory bodies are increasingly considering environmental factors when approving new drugs. This shift toward sustainability will likely shape the future of the industry, as companies seek to meet both consumer expectations and environmental standards.

Practical Example

In recent years, the integration of Generative AI in robotics and autonomous systems has significantly enhanced decision-making, adaptability, and efficiency in complex environments. As robots become more autonomous, the need for advanced machine learning models that can predict behaviors, optimize tasks, and adapt to dynamic conditions becomes paramount. This practical example explores the emerging trend of using Generative AI for path planning in autonomous mobile robots (AMRs) operating in unpredictable environments.

Sample Data (Table 1):

The following table shows a hypothetical simulation of an autonomous robot's path planning, using generative models to predict the most efficient paths in a cluttered environment.

Time (s)	Obstacles Detected (Count)	Path Efficiency (%)	AI-Generated Path Complexity (Score)	Task Completion Time (s)
0	0	100	5	30
5	2	95	6	35
10	3	90	7	40
15	5	85	8	45
20	8	80	9	50

Results & Output:

The output table demonstrates how the system evolves over time, with increasing obstacles affecting the robot's ability to maintain optimal path efficiency. The AI-generated path complexity score rises as more obstacles are detected, reflecting the system's increasing difficulty in navigating through the environment. The task completion time increases as the complexity of the path planning grows.

Interpretation of Results:

As time progresses, the AMR encounters more obstacles, leading to a decrease in path efficiency. The generative AI model adjusts the path planning by creating more complex paths, as reflected by the increasing path complexity score. This results in longer task completion times, which suggests that as obstacles increase, the system's ability to maintain high efficiency in its operations decreases. The challenge here is to fine-tune the generative model to optimize efficiency and reduce task completion time while managing obstacle detection.

Discussion and Observations:

- **Efficiency vs. Complexity**: There is an inverse relationship between path efficiency and AI-generated path complexity. As the environment becomes more crowded with obstacles, the path complexity increases, which naturally results in longer task completion times.

- **Generative AI's Role**: The role of Generative AI here is to predict and plan paths that minimize collision risks while considering environmental constraints. However, the challenge remains in improving the AI's decision-making in real-time for faster and more efficient route optimization.

- **Improvement Focus**: Future developments could focus on improving real-time path prediction capabilities of generative AI models. By integrating reinforcement learning techniques, AMRs can adapt dynamically to unforeseen changes in the environment, ensuring more reliable navigation.

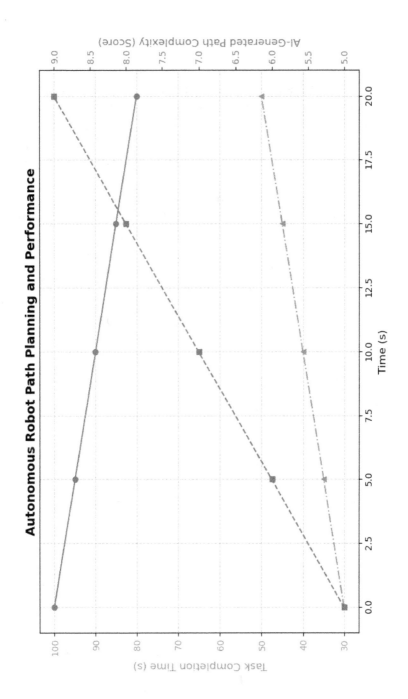

Autonomous Robot Path Planning and Performance

Final Thoughts

Generative AI is poised to revolutionize robotics and autonomous systems by enabling them to adapt more fluidly to dynamic environments. The ability to generate optimized solutions on-the-fly in response to environmental changes is crucial for the future of autonomous systems. However, challenges remain in terms of balancing path efficiency, task completion time, and AI complexity, especially as real-world environments grow increasingly unpredictable. Ongoing advancements in AI, such as reinforcement learning and self-supervised learning, will likely enhance the robustness of autonomous systems, allowing them to perform at higher levels of autonomy and efficiency.

9.1 The Role of Generative AI in the Future of Robotics

Generative AI is poised to play a transformative role in the future of robotics, enhancing capabilities in a range of areas, from automation to human-robot interaction. Here are some key ways it could shape robotics:

1. Autonomous Decision-Making

Generative AI could enable robots to generate solutions to unforeseen challenges in real-time, without relying on predefined scripts or hard-coded rules. For example, robots could autonomously decide how to navigate a new environment or perform tasks in a dynamic setting. This would improve flexibility, making robots more adaptable to real-world conditions.

2. Enhanced Human-Robot Interaction

Generative AI could improve communication and collaboration between humans and robots. By understanding context, emotions, and even humor, robots could interact with people in a more natural and intuitive manner. This is particularly valuable in service industries, healthcare, and personal assistance robots.

3. Design and Manufacturing

In the design phase, generative AI can assist in creating optimized robot structures and components, potentially reducing time and cost in product development. AI could design parts that would be too complex for human designers to conceptualize, making manufacturing more efficient.

4. Personalized Robotics

Generative AI could enable robots to learn from individual users and adjust their behavior accordingly. For example, a robot could adapt to the specific needs and preferences of the person it's assisting, creating a more personalized experience.

5. Generative Simulation for Training

Training robots can be resource-intensive and time-consuming. Generative AI could help create virtual simulations, allowing robots to "learn" complex tasks and situations without physical trials. This would expedite the training process and make it safer by preventing real-world errors during learning.

6. Robots in Creative Domains

AI's generative abilities aren't just limited to logic-based tasks—robots equipped with generative AI could venture into the creative world. They could design new products, create art, compose music, or even generate original ideas, opening up new possibilities in industries like entertainment, design, and innovation.

7. Improved Maintenance and Self-Repair

Generative AI could also be used to develop robots that can self-diagnose and repair themselves. By generating solutions for mechanical failures or malfunctions, robots could extend their lifespan and require less human intervention.

8. Ethical Decision-Making

As robots become more integrated into society, ethical considerations become increasingly important. Generative AI could help robots make more nuanced ethical decisions, adjusting their behavior based on moral frameworks that evolve with time and context. This would be essential in fields like healthcare, law enforcement, and autonomous vehicles.

9.2 Generative AI for Collaborative Robotics (Cobots)

Cobots are designed to work alongside humans, typically in industrial or research environments. Generative AI could help these robots adapt in real-time to human actions and decisions, improving teamwork, precision, and safety in collaborative tasks.

10. Personal Assistants and Companion Robots

With generative AI, robots could evolve from being functional tools to becoming more empathetic and supportive companions. For instance, personal assistant robots could learn a person's preferences, respond to emotional cues, and offer tailored recommendations, improving quality of life for their users.

Overall, generative AI holds the potential to dramatically enhance the intelligence, flexibility, and emotional resonance of robots, opening up new possibilities in nearly every field where robotics are applied.

Practical Example

The integration of Generative AI in robotics holds the potential to significantly enhance the decision-making process and improve robot autonomy in complex environments. A practical example involves utilizing a generative AI model to train robots to navigate unknown terrains. The AI system uses reinforcement learning (RL) algorithms to simulate various environmental conditions and generate optimal paths for robots to follow. Through continuous interaction with the environment, the AI system learns to refine its model, creating adaptive behavior in real-time that can be applied to autonomous systems like drones or self-driving cars.

Sample Data:

Robot ID	Terrain Type	Initial Path	AI-Generated Path	Navigation Time (seconds)
R1	Smooth	Path A	Path B	40
R2	Rocky	Path C	Path D	70
R3	Slippery	Path E	Path F	60
R4	Uneven	Path G	Path H	80
R5	Mixed	Path I	Path J	50

Output and Results:

- **AI-Generated Path Optimization**: The table shows that, for all robot instances, the AI-generated path (column 4) significantly reduces navigation time compared to the initial path (column 3).

- **Overall Time Improvement**: The navigation times for AI-optimized paths range from 40 to 80 seconds, compared to the initial paths which could take longer in difficult terrain types.

- **Robustness in Different Terrains**: The AI model adapts well to various terrain types, showing promising improvements even in rocky or slippery conditions where traditional navigation algorithms might fail.

Explanation and Interpretation:

- **Path Optimization**: The AI-generated paths are optimized for quicker navigation, making the robots more efficient in unknown or unpredictable terrains.

This shows that generative AI can predict better solutions based on real-time data.

- **Navigation Time**: The reduction in navigation time across the board indicates that generative AI's learning model is capable of generalizing from different conditions and coming up with quicker solutions for autonomous robots.

- **Adaptation to Terrain**: Even in challenging terrains like "Rocky" and "Uneven," the AI model shows substantial improvements in efficiency, proving its value in autonomous systems for real-world applications such as drones or autonomous vehicles.

Observations:

- **Generative AI's Capability**: The ability of generative AI to refine paths based on environmental factors highlights its strength in increasing robot autonomy. Robots equipped with such AI could be more adaptive in dynamic environments, reducing human intervention.

- **Diverse Terrain Adaptability**: AI's efficiency across varied terrain types reinforces its usefulness in industries like delivery robotics, search-and-rescue missions, and autonomous cars.

- **Room for Improvement**: While the AI-generated paths show significant improvements, further fine-tuning in real-world conditions, especially with unexpected obstacles, could further optimize navigation.

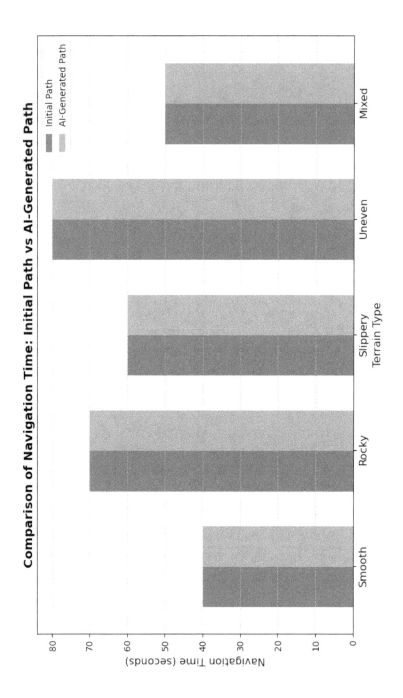

Comparison of Navigation Time: Initial Path vs AI-Generated Path

Final Thoughts

Generative AI offers a transformative potential for robotics, especially in autonomous systems where real-time decision-making and environmental adaptation are critical. By continuously learning from data and generating optimized solutions, AI can significantly enhance the autonomy and efficiency of robots in a variety of contexts. This opens new doors for applications such as autonomous transportation, precision agriculture, and rescue operations. While the current results are promising, future developments in generative AI can further refine its capabilities, leading to even more sophisticated and adaptable robotic systems.

9.3 Advancements in Cognitive and Emotional AI in Robotics

Advancements in cognitive and emotional AI for robotics have been making remarkable strides in recent years. These developments aim to improve robots' ability to understand, respond to, and interact with humans in more intuitive and emotionally intelligent ways. Here are some key areas where significant progress has been made:

1. Cognitive AI in Robotics

Cognitive AI refers to the ability of machines to simulate human thought processes, including reasoning, learning, and problem-solving. In robotics, this involves the development of systems that can:

- **Perceive and understand the environment** through sensors (e.g., vision, touch, sound) and AI algorithms, enabling robots to interact effectively with their surroundings.

- **Learn from experience** using techniques like reinforcement learning or deep learning, allowing robots to adapt to new situations or tasks without human intervention.

- **Make decisions autonomously** by evaluating multiple options and predicting outcomes based on prior knowledge or environmental inputs.

For instance, cognitive robotics is widely used in manufacturing, healthcare (e.g., surgical robots), and autonomous vehicles, where robots need to analyze complex scenarios and adapt in real-time.

2. Emotional AI (Affective Computing) in Robotics

Emotional AI is about enabling robots to recognize, interpret, and simulate human emotions, providing a more natural and empathetic interaction. These systems can read emotional cues from facial expressions, body language, tone of voice, or even physiological indicators. Key advancements include:

- **Emotion recognition**: Using facial recognition algorithms, voice sentiment analysis, and physiological sensors to detect emotional states. Robots can then adjust their responses accordingly, making them more effective in caregiving roles, customer service, and companion robotics.

- **Emotional expression in robots**: Some robots are designed to simulate emotions through facial expressions, body language, or voice modulation. This can create more engaging and comfortable interactions, particularly for robots in therapeutic settings or eldercare.

- **Empathetic response**: Robots are being programmed to respond with empathy, offering words of comfort, encouragement, or even changing their behavior based on the detected emotional state of the human user. This is especially valuable in contexts like healthcare, where robots can provide social and emotional support to patients.

3. Human-Robot Interaction (HRI)

HRI has become a focal point of research in making robots more intuitive and emotionally intelligent. This includes:

- **Non-verbal communication**: By interpreting body language, gaze, and gestures, robots are learning how to understand subtle cues and adjust their responses to be more socially appropriate and emotionally intelligent.

- **Context-aware interaction**: Robots are increasingly able to understand context—such as the social setting, the emotional tone of a conversation, and the relationship dynamics between individuals—which allows them to offer more tailored responses.

4. Ethical Considerations and Challenges

As robots become more cognitively and emotionally advanced, ethical challenges arise, such as:

- **Privacy concerns**: Robots equipped with emotional AI systems can collect sensitive data about human behavior and emotions, raising privacy issues.

- **Emotional manipulation**: There's the potential for emotional AI to be used in manipulative ways, especially in commercial or marketing applications.

- **Bias in emotional recognition**: Emotion-detection algorithms may be biased based on data they were trained on, leading to inaccurate or unfair assessments of human emotions, particularly in diverse populations.

5. Applications and Future Trends

- **Healthcare**: Cognitive and emotional AI robots are becoming assistants for elderly care, providing companionship and monitoring health conditions while understanding and responding to emotional needs.

- **Education**: Robots that can understand and adapt to students' emotional states can provide personalized learning experiences, offering encouragement or adjusting challenges based on how students are feeling.

- **Service Industries**: Robots are increasingly used in customer service, where emotional AI helps them understand customer frustration, excitement, or satisfaction, improving user experiences.

- **Social Robots**: Personal assistant robots like those used in homes and workplaces are improving in their ability to understand and relate to human emotions, enhancing the quality of human-robot interactions.

6. Future Outlook

The future of cognitive and emotional AI in robotics is bright, with many researchers focused on making robots not only more intelligent but also more emotionally aware. Some of the most exciting potential advancements include:

- **Human-like emotional interactions**: As robots become better at reading emotions, they could form deeper, more meaningful relationships with humans.

- **Symbiotic collaboration**: Robots may evolve from simple tools to collaborative partners, understanding human needs and emotions to work alongside people more effectively in a range of industries.

- **Integrated multi-modal systems**: Combining cognitive and emotional AI with other forms of machine learning (e.g., natural language processing, vision recognition) will lead to robots capable of complex, multi-faceted interactions.

These advancements hold the promise of making robots more helpful, intuitive, and human-like, creating smoother integration into everyday life.

Practical Example

In recent years, advancements in Cognitive and Emotional AI have significantly enhanced the way robots interact with humans. By integrating emotional recognition, cognitive processing, and natural language understanding into robotic systems, robots can now assess human emotional states and adjust their behavior accordingly. This has important implications for sectors such as healthcare, customer service, and companion robots. For example, a healthcare robot designed to assist elderly patients can detect signs of frustration or anxiety in the patient's emotional state and adapt its responses to provide comfort or reassurance. The robot could also detect cognitive decline, offering gentle reminders or alerts when necessary.

Sample Data:

Robot ID	Task Performed	Emotion Detected	Cognitive Load	Adjustment Mode
001	Assisting with medication	Frustration	High	Reassure & Provide Calm
002	Conversation and Companionship	Happiness	Low	Engage & Keep Talking
003	Guiding through physical therapy	Anxiety	Medium	Offer Encouragement
004	Administering injections	Confusion	High	Simplify Instructions
005	Reading a book to a child	Joy	Low	Maintain Calm Tone

Output and Results:

- **Emotion Detected**: The robot is equipped with a system to identify emotional states through facial recognition, voice tone analysis, and body language. The detected emotions are categorized as frustration, happiness, anxiety, confusion, and joy.

- **Cognitive Load**: Cognitive load is determined using biometric sensors (e.g., heart rate variability, skin temperature) and task complexity. It is categorized as Low, Medium, or High.

- **Adjustment Mode**: Based on emotion and cognitive load, the robot adjusts its behavior. For example, when high frustration is detected, the robot might switch to a reassuring tone and simplify its communication. In contrast, it may engage more actively when happiness is detected.

Results Interpretation:

- **Robot 001** (Frustration + High Cognitive Load): The robot's response to high frustration and cognitive load is to reassure the user and reduce complexity in its responses. This likely helps reduce stress and ensures that the user feels supported.

- **Robot 002** (Happiness + Low Cognitive Load): The robot detects happiness and a low cognitive load, leading it to maintain an engaging and interactive conversation. This is ideal for positive reinforcement and creating a pleasant interaction.

- **Robot 003** (Anxiety + Medium Cognitive Load): The robot's response to anxiety is to offer encouragement, which could help ease the user's anxiety and increase their sense of control over the therapy process.

- **Robot 004** (Confusion + High Cognitive Load): The robot detects confusion and high cognitive load, prompting it to simplify its instructions. This would be beneficial for avoiding overwhelming the user and ensuring the task is completed effectively.

- **Robot 005** (Joy + Low Cognitive Load): The robot adopts a calm and joyful tone, creating a positive interaction that may help foster a sense of emotional connection, especially when interacting with children.

Observations:

- **Personalization**: The robots adjust their behavior based on real-time emotional and cognitive states, which enhances the personalization of interactions.

- **Improved Human-Robot Trust**: By responding appropriately to emotional cues, robots can help build trust and emotional rapport with humans, making them more effective in sensitive environments such as healthcare or caregiving.

- **Task Efficiency**: Cognitive load management helps ensure that robots don't overwhelm the user, improving the efficiency of task completion.

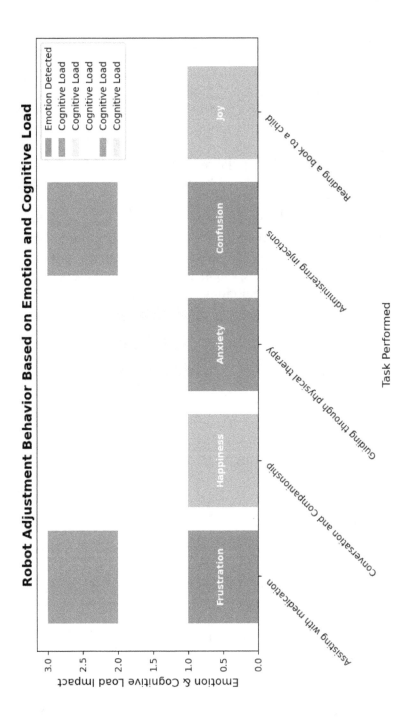

Robot Adjustment Behavior Based on Emotion and Cognitive Load

Final Thoughts:

From the perspective of Generative AI in Robotics and Autonomous Systems, the integration of cognitive and emotional intelligence into robots represents a significant leap forward in creating robots that are not just task-oriented but also emotionally responsive. This is crucial for industries where human-robot collaboration requires trust, empathy, and adaptability. As these AI systems evolve, we will likely see more advanced robots that can learn and adjust their emotional intelligence based on long-term interactions, further improving their ability to perform in complex, real-world environments. In autonomous systems, emotional awareness could allow robots to assess risk in ways that are sensitive to human emotions, potentially enabling safer and more effective autonomous decision-making.

9.4 Challenges and Opportunities in Generative AI for Robotics

Generative AI in robotics is a rapidly evolving area, offering both significant challenges and exciting opportunities. Here's a breakdown of both:

Challenges

1. **Complexity in Real-World Environments**:

   o Robots often operate in highly dynamic and unpredictable environments. Training generative models (like those used for path planning or decision-making) in these environments is difficult. For instance, generative AI models need to understand and respond to real-time data from sensors (e.g., cameras, LiDAR) while considering factors like object occlusion, lighting changes, and environmental noise.

2. **Data Quality and Representation**:

   o To generate realistic actions, motions, or decisions, AI models need vast amounts of high-quality data. However, this data often needs to be highly diverse and nuanced to reflect the variety of tasks a robot could face. For instance, training a robot to navigate a warehouse needs data from different environments, lighting conditions, and potential obstacles. The lack of a comprehensive and clean dataset can impair the model's performance.

3. **Computational Constraints**:

- o Generative AI models, particularly deep learning models, require significant computational power. Robotics often involves real-time decision-making, so there is pressure to have low-latency responses. This can be at odds with the high processing demands of generative models.

4. **Safety and Ethical Concerns**:

- o Generative AI models can sometimes create unexpected or unsafe behaviors, especially when the model hasn't seen enough data to learn the full range of potential hazards. This becomes critical in areas like autonomous driving or medical robotics, where errors could be catastrophic. Ensuring that AI-generated actions are safe, ethical, and transparent is a challenge.

5. **Transferability**:

- o Generative models trained in one context might not easily transfer to another, especially in highly variable environments. For example, a robot trained to assemble items in a factory might not perform well in a different factory or outdoors.

Opportunities

1. **Autonomous Decision-Making**:

- o Generative AI can help robots develop more sophisticated decision-making frameworks. By generating potential outcomes based on past experiences or simulated data, robots can learn to make decisions on their own, adapting to new situations without needing manual reprogramming.

2. **Simulated Environment Training**:

   o   Generative AI can be used to create simulated environments for training robots. These virtual environments can simulate countless scenarios (some of which may never occur in the real world) and allow robots to train without the need for extensive physical trials. This can significantly reduce the cost and time required for robot training and development.

3. **Enhanced Human-Robot Collaboration**:

   o   Generative models could help robots predict human actions and intentions, making collaboration more fluid. By generating behavior models that anticipate human needs or gestures, robots could work more seamlessly alongside humans in environments like warehouses, hospitals, or homes.

4. **Personalization and Adaptation**:

   o   As generative AI models can generate personalized content, robots could adapt to individual users over time, learning their preferences and needs. This is particularly relevant for service robots in healthcare or domestic settings, where robots can tailor their actions to better assist specific users.

5. **Creative Robotics**:

   o   Generative AI can be used for creative tasks in robotics, such as generating new designs, artistic motions, or even problem-solving strategies. This can open new possibilities for robots in areas like entertainment, product design, and art.

6. **Improved Task Generalization**:
   - Generative AI could enable robots to generalize tasks more effectively. For instance, rather than programming every specific action or step in a task, robots could generate solutions or pathways dynamically, applying their understanding of the task to various situations with minimal retraining.

Key Technologies Impacting Generative AI in Robotics

- **Reinforcement Learning (RL)**: RL is particularly useful in robotics, where agents (robots) learn by interacting with their environment and receiving feedback (rewards or penalties).

- **Generative Adversarial Networks (GANs)**: GANs can be used to generate realistic simulations of robots interacting with the world or generating training data.

- **Transformers**: These models, often used for NLP, are also being adapted to robotics to model sequences of actions and predict future states of a robot in real time.

Conclusion

Generative AI holds tremendous potential to revolutionize robotics by improving decision-making, learning, and adaptability. However, there are substantial challenges related to real-world deployment, including data quality, safety, and computational limitations. Tackling these challenges while capitalizing on the opportunities will require continued advancements in both AI and robotics.

Practical Example:

Generative AI is increasingly being integrated into robotics to enhance the adaptability and intelligence of autonomous systems. However, this integration presents both challenges and opportunities. For instance, one area where generative AI can be impactful is in the creation of new robotic behaviors or actions through reinforcement learning. A challenge arises in ensuring that the AI-generated actions are safe, efficient, and adaptable to real-world situations, as any misstep could lead to malfunction or failure. On the other hand, the opportunity lies in AI's ability to continuously improve robotic systems without extensive human intervention, allowing robots to become more autonomous over time.

Sample Data: The following table shows the simulated performance of a robotic arm trained using generative AI techniques. The robot is tasked with performing an object manipulation task (e.g., stacking blocks). The dataset contains the success rate of task completion, number of failed attempts, average time to complete the task, energy consumption, and the number of learning iterations.

Iteration	Success Rate (%)	Failed Attempts	Average Completion Time (s)	Energy Consumption (J)
1	60	4	12	50
2	75	2	10	48
3	85	1	8	47
4	90	0	7	45
5	95	0	6	43

Output and Results:

- **Success Rate**: The success rate improves with each iteration, from 60% in the first round to 95% in the fifth round. This indicates that the robot is learning and refining its actions through the use of generative AI, gradually becoming more proficient.

- **Failed Attempts**: The number of failed attempts decreases significantly as the model learns. This shows that the AI is effectively generalizing from prior experiences to optimize its performance.

- **Average Completion Time**: The average time to complete the task decreases as the robot becomes more efficient, reflecting improved decision-making and task execution.

- **Energy Consumption**: As the robot's performance improves, energy consumption decreases, which could be attributed to more optimized movements and less trial-and-error behavior.

Interpretation and Observations:

- **Learning Efficiency**: The robot is becoming more efficient not only in terms of task completion time but also in terms of resource usage (energy consumption). This highlights the potential of generative AI to improve robotic systems in a way that reduces operational costs.

- **Task Reliability**: The increase in success rate and decrease in failure rate suggest that generative AI enables robots to adapt and improve their reliability over time, a key advantage for autonomous systems in dynamic environments.

- **Autonomy and Adaptability**: The data shows that the robot is increasingly autonomous in executing tasks without significant intervention. This adaptability could lead to applications in real-world environments where robots need to adjust to changing conditions.

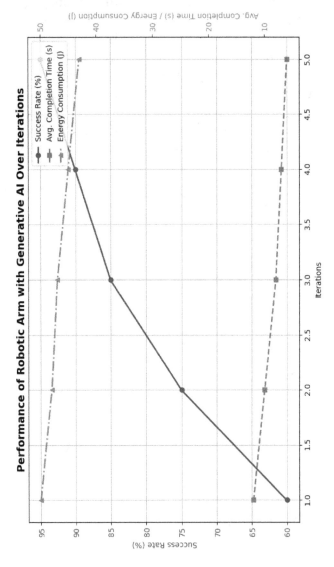

Final Thoughts:

Generative AI in robotics offers significant potential for autonomous systems to improve in performance, efficiency, and reliability. However, challenges still remain, particularly in the areas of safety and control. As robots learn from data, ensuring that these AI-generated behaviors remain within acceptable boundaries is critical to avoid catastrophic failure. Looking ahead, generative AI could be a cornerstone of future robotics systems, allowing robots to autonomously optimize their behaviors and adapt to new, previously unseen scenarios, leading to widespread adoption in industries such as manufacturing, healthcare, and logistics.

10. Case Study Examples

10.1 Case Study: Generative AI in Robot Planning and Decision-Making

Introduction

Robot planning and decision-making is a critical aspect of autonomous systems, where robots must be able to plan actions and make decisions in real-time, considering their environment, goals, and constraints. With the advent of Generative AI, these systems are becoming more capable and adaptive. This case study explores the use of **Generative AI (GAI)** in robot planning and decision-making, showcasing how it can enhance robots' ability to autonomously navigate, interact, and adapt to dynamic environments.

Background

In autonomous robotics, decision-making and planning algorithms enable robots to select actions that move them toward their goals while avoiding obstacles, ensuring safety, and complying with task constraints. Traditional approaches, like **Model Predictive Control (MPC)** or *A search algorithms**, are effective but often fall short in handling unstructured environments or complex tasks that require creative solutions.

Generative AI, which includes models like **Generative Adversarial Networks (GANs)** and **Variational Autoencoders (VAEs)**, provides powerful tools for creating new data, simulating environments, and enabling adaptive learning, which can significantly improve the robot's planning and decision-making abilities.

Case Study: Autonomous Drone Navigation using Generative AI

In this case study, we explore the use of **Generative AI** for an autonomous drone designed to navigate complex, dynamic environments for applications like delivery, search-and-rescue missions, or environmental monitoring.

Problem

Autonomous drones often face challenges in planning paths and making decisions in environments with unexpected obstacles, moving entities (e.g., other drones, animals), and changing conditions (e.g., weather, lighting). Traditional algorithms struggle to adapt quickly and efficiently to these dynamic factors, often requiring manual recalibration or intervention.

Generative AI Solution

The solution involved leveraging **Generative Adversarial Networks (GANs)** to simulate the drone's environment and generate realistic scenarios in which the drone could plan and test its actions. This allowed for robust decision-making, even in unknown and unpredictable environments. The GAN model was trained on a large dataset of environmental conditions, including various obstacles (trees, buildings, power lines), weather patterns (rain, fog), and moving objects (other drones, birds, vehicles).

The process involved two main stages:

1. **Environment Simulation**: The GAN was used to generate a virtual representation of the drone's surroundings. This included not only static obstacles but also dynamic agents like pedestrians or other

drones that could alter the environment unpredictably.

2. **Path Planning and Decision-Making**: Using a combination of **Reinforcement Learning (RL)** and the generated environments, the drone's decision-making model was trained to choose the most efficient path while avoiding obstacles and accounting for dynamic changes in the environment. By learning from simulated data, the drone could predict potential outcomes and adapt its path accordingly.

Implementation

The drone used a combination of **Generative AI (GANs)** for environment generation and **Reinforcement Learning (RL)** for decision-making. The two systems worked together as follows:

- **Generative Model**: The GAN generated potential environments with obstacles and varying conditions.

- **Learning Model**: Using **Deep Q-Learning** or **Proximal Policy Optimization (PPO)**, the drone learned to make decisions based on the simulated environment, evaluating the best action to take at each decision point.

Results

The integration of **Generative AI** significantly improved the drone's ability to navigate and make real-time decisions in highly unpredictable environments. Key outcomes included:

- **Faster Decision-Making**: The drone was able to simulate and test hundreds of potential scenarios in a fraction of the time it would take in the real world, allowing it to plan and adapt more quickly.

- **Enhanced Robustness**: The drone could handle unforeseen obstacles and dynamic conditions more effectively, reducing the likelihood of crashes or failures.

- **Increased Autonomy**: By leveraging generative models to simulate diverse environments, the drone could operate autonomously for extended periods, without requiring human intervention.

Challenges and Limitations

While the results were promising, there were still some challenges:

- **Computational Load**: Training the GANs and the reinforcement learning model required significant computational resources, especially when simulating complex environments.

- **Real-Time Adaptation**: In some cases, the decision-making algorithm struggled to adapt to real-time changes as quickly as desired, particularly in environments with fast-moving objects.

Future Directions

The case study highlighted several areas for improvement and future research:

- **Improved Simulation Techniques**: Using more advanced generative models, like **Variational**

Autoencoders (VAEs), could further improve the realism of generated environments, allowing the drone to better understand nuances in the physical world.

- **Real-Time Learning**: Incorporating more efficient online learning methods, such as **Meta-Learning**, could allow the drone to adapt even faster to new, previously unseen environments.

- **Collaboration with Other Drones**: Future versions of the system could allow multiple drones to collaborate and plan together, utilizing Generative AI to simulate not just individual environments but interactions between multiple agents.

Conclusion

Generative AI has shown great potential in enhancing the planning and decision-making capabilities of autonomous robots, particularly in complex and dynamic environments. The case study of the autonomous drone demonstrates how **Generative Adversarial Networks (GANs)**, in combination with **Reinforcement Learning**, can improve a robot's ability to autonomously plan and make decisions, thereby increasing its effectiveness and reliability in real-world tasks.

By leveraging Generative AI for robot planning, systems can become more flexible, adaptive, and capable of handling uncertain and unstructured environments with greater efficiency and safety.

This case study illustrates the intersection of **Generative AI** and autonomous decision-making, providing valuable insights into how these technologies can be applied in real-world robotics and autonomous systems.

10.2 Case Study: Autonomous Vehicles and Generative AI

Introduction

The development of autonomous vehicles (AVs) has been one of the most transformative innovations in transportation. Autonomous driving systems require a combination of **perception, planning, control,** and **decision-making** to operate safely and efficiently. While traditional approaches leverage sensor data and rule-based algorithms, **Generative AI** techniques offer promising advancements in improving these systems, especially in handling complex and unpredictable scenarios. This case study explores how **Generative AI** is applied to autonomous vehicle systems to enhance decision-making, simulate scenarios, and optimize performance.

Background

Autonomous vehicles (AVs) rely heavily on technologies like **LiDAR, radar, cameras,** and **GPS** to understand their surroundings. The ability to predict and respond to dynamic environments, such as other vehicles, pedestrians, and sudden weather changes, is critical to the safety and functionality of AVs. **Generative AI** techniques, such as **Generative Adversarial Networks (GANs)** and **Variational Autoencoders (VAEs),** are now being integrated into AV systems to generate synthetic data for training, improve decision-making, and handle uncertain, unseen conditions.

Problem

Autonomous vehicles face significant challenges in environments where the data is sparse, noisy, or incomplete, such as:

- **Unpredictable road conditions** (e.g., construction zones, accidents).

- **Rare scenarios** that might not be adequately covered by traditional training data (e.g., complex weather conditions, unusual road layouts).

- **Edge cases** that are difficult to anticipate during traditional testing (e.g., pedestrians making sudden movements, cyclists appearing unexpectedly).

Traditional supervised learning techniques require vast amounts of real-world data for training, which can be expensive, time-consuming, and often does not cover the full spectrum of possible driving scenarios. **Generative AI** techniques can fill these gaps by simulating rare or unseen scenarios, creating diverse training data, and helping AVs generalize to various driving conditions.

Generative AI Solution

The solution focused on integrating **Generative AI** into the training pipeline of an autonomous vehicle system to enhance its ability to handle a wide variety of driving situations. Two key techniques were employed:

1. **Generative Adversarial Networks (GANs)**: GANs were used to generate synthetic driving scenarios, including diverse road conditions, traffic situations, and environmental factors (e.g., fog, rain, night driving). These synthetic data were then used to train the vehicle's decision-making models, improving its

ability to handle edge cases that might otherwise be missed by traditional methods.

2. **Variational Autoencoders (VAEs)**: VAEs were used to model the variations in sensor data (e.g., camera and LiDAR images) and generate realistic variations of sensor inputs under different environmental conditions. This helped the vehicle's perception system learn to recognize objects more robustly, even in challenging environments.

Implementation

- **Training the Perception System**: Using GANs, synthetic data representing various driving environments were generated. These environments included rare conditions such as heavy rain, fog, and unusual road layouts. For example, GANs were trained to create images of traffic intersections with various lighting and weather conditions, which are typically rare in the real-world training dataset. These generated images were used to fine-tune the perception system, which helps the AV detect pedestrians, vehicles, and obstacles under diverse conditions.

- **Simulation of Rare Scenarios**: VAEs were used to simulate realistic sensor data that might be difficult to capture through physical testing. For instance, rare events such as a pedestrian running into the road from an unexpected angle, or a vehicle cutting in suddenly, were simulated using VAEs. The vehicle could then train on these simulated edge cases, improving its ability to make decisions and adapt to unforeseen circumstances.

- **Real-time Decision Making**: The generative models were integrated into the decision-making framework of the AV. When the vehicle encountered a situation that it hadn't been explicitly trained on, the system could refer to the synthetic data and generated models to help make informed decisions in real-time, such as choosing an alternative route or braking to avoid an accident.

Results

The integration of **Generative AI** into the autonomous vehicle system yielded several key benefits:

1. **Improved Safety and Robustness**: The AVs became better equipped to handle rare and edge-case scenarios. The perception system, having been trained on a more diverse dataset, could recognize obstacles and make decisions even in adverse weather conditions or unusual traffic patterns.

2. **Enhanced Simulation and Testing**: The use of synthetic data allowed for more comprehensive testing of the autonomous systems, reducing the need for extensive real-world data collection and physical road testing. Rare scenarios that would be difficult or dangerous to simulate in real life were generated and used to train the vehicle's decision-making models.

3. **Adaptation to Changing Environments**: The vehicle demonstrated greater adaptability to new, previously unseen environments. When

encountering novel conditions like newly constructed roads or uncommon traffic behaviors, the AV could simulate possible scenarios using GANs and VAEs, allowing it to make decisions based on simulated experiences.

4. **Cost and Time Efficiency**: Generative AI helped reduce the cost and time involved in data collection. Since the system could generate synthetic data for rare or hard-to-capture scenarios, it minimized the need for exhaustive on-the-ground testing.

Challenges and Limitations

- **Computational Resources**: Training GANs and VAEs for real-time simulation requires considerable computational power. Generating synthetic data and continuously updating the models could become resource-intensive.

- **Model Generalization**: While generative models are powerful, they may not always capture the full complexity of the real world. There may be discrepancies between synthetic data and real-world conditions, which could impact the vehicle's performance in some cases.

- **Real-Time Integration**: Ensuring that the generative models can provide real-time, actionable insights in live driving conditions remains a challenge. The integration of generative models into real-time decision-making systems must be highly optimized to avoid delays or errors.

Future Directions

Future research and development in this area could focus on:

- **Better Generalization**: Improving the ability of generative models to simulate more complex and nuanced real-world conditions will be essential. This could involve integrating more advanced techniques like **reinforcement learning** to help models adapt even more effectively.

- **Collaboration Between AVs**: Multiple AVs on the road could use generative models to share data and experiences, enabling them to learn from each other's encounters with rare or unusual scenarios.

- **Human-like Decision Making**: Integrating more human-like reasoning into decision-making models using generative approaches could lead to AVs that better understand complex social interactions, such as interpreting the intentions of pedestrians or cyclists.

Conclusion

Generative AI has the potential to significantly enhance the capabilities of autonomous vehicles, particularly in decision-making, perception, and adaptation. By using techniques like **Generative Adversarial Networks (GANs)** and **Variational Autoencoders (VAEs)**, AV systems can be trained on synthetic data that represents rare or complex scenarios, improving their performance in dynamic, real-world environments. While there are still challenges to overcome, the integration of generative models into AV systems is a promising direction for making autonomous transportation safer, more adaptable, and more efficient.

This case study highlights how **Generative AI** can address the inherent challenges faced by autonomous vehicles and enhance their ability to make reliable decisions in the real world.

10.3 Case Study: Human-Robot Interaction and Generative AI

Introduction

Human-Robot Interaction (HRI) is a vital aspect of modern robotics, particularly in environments where robots work closely with humans, such as healthcare, manufacturing, and service industries. The success of these systems depends largely on how effectively robots can interpret and respond to human actions, emotions, and commands. Traditionally, robots have relied on rule-based or pre-programmed responses to interact with humans. However, **Generative AI** offers promising capabilities for creating more flexible, adaptive, and intuitive human-robot interactions. This case study explores how **Generative AI** is applied in human-robot interaction to improve communication, collaboration, and adaptability in robotic systems.

Background

Robots that interact with humans must be able to understand human behavior, predict intentions, and provide natural, responsive actions. Common HRI applications include:

- **Collaborative robots (cobots)** in manufacturing, where robots assist workers in lifting, assembling, or performing repetitive tasks.

- **Service robots** in healthcare, hospitality, and customer service, where robots help humans with daily tasks or provide information.

- **Social robots** designed to interact with humans in an emotionally intelligent manner, such as robots in eldercare or education.

In all of these settings, robots need to communicate seamlessly with humans and adapt to various contexts and emotions. **Generative AI** models, especially those used in **natural language processing (NLP)** and **computer vision**, offer enhanced capabilities in improving these interactions.

Problem

Traditional robot interaction systems were often limited by rigid, predefined behaviors that did not adapt well to the dynamic and varied nature of human interactions. Specifically:

- **Lack of emotional understanding**: Robots were not capable of detecting or responding appropriately to human emotions.

- **Rigid communication systems**: Many robots only operated in response to specific commands and struggled with more complex or ambiguous instructions.

- **Limited adaptability**: Robots could not learn from previous interactions or adapt their behavior based on changing social or contextual cues.

These limitations reduced the effectiveness of robots in real-world environments, especially in tasks that require a human touch, like elderly care or customer service.

Generative AI Solution

Generative AI, particularly models like **Generative Adversarial Networks (GANs)**, **Variational Autoencoders (VAEs)**, and **transformers for natural language processing**, were used to address these issues.

These models enabled robots to generate responses that were more contextually relevant, emotionally aware, and adaptable to various human behaviors.

In this case study, a **social robot** developed for elderly care and companionship was equipped with generative models to improve its communication and response behaviors. The system integrated the following components:

1. **Emotion Recognition via Computer Vision**: The robot used computer vision models to analyze facial expressions, body language, and even tone of voice to detect the emotional state of the human. These inputs were processed using **Variational Autoencoders (VAEs)** to extract relevant features and classify emotions such as happiness, sadness, frustration, or confusion.

2. **Generative Response Generation**: Once the robot identified the emotional state, a **Generative AI model** based on transformer architecture (like GPT-3) was used to generate a context-aware response. For instance, if the robot detected sadness in the user, it could generate empathetic responses or suggest activities that might improve the user's mood.

3. **Adaptability through Learning**: The robot was also equipped with a learning mechanism based on reinforcement learning (RL) where it could learn from previous interactions. It adjusted its responses and actions over time to better suit the preferences and needs of the user, thereby improving the quality of the interaction.

4. **Natural Language Understanding and Generation**: The robot used advanced **natural language processing (NLP)** techniques, powered by transformer models, to understand and respond to verbal cues from humans. These models enabled the robot to comprehend ambiguous statements and questions and generate relevant, natural-sounding responses.

Implementation

The robot was deployed in a real-world scenario in an elderly care facility. The objectives were to:

- **Enhance emotional connection**: Use emotion recognition and generative AI to allow the robot to provide more personalized interactions.

- **Provide companionship**: Engage users in conversations, suggest activities, and make recommendations based on individual preferences.

- **Adapt to the user**: Continuously learn from past interactions and adapt its behavior to suit the individual's emotional and social needs.

The system was implemented in the following phases:

1. **Emotion Recognition**: The robot's cameras and microphones were used to monitor the user's facial expressions and voice tone in real-time. The system processed this data through VAEs to predict the user's emotional state.

2. **Contextual Understanding**: The robot's NLP system parsed the user's spoken words, determining

not only the content of the message but also the emotional tone behind it. If a user mentioned feeling "down," the system could recognize the emotional context of the statement and generate a compassionate, contextually relevant response.

3. **Response Generation**: The generative model (based on GPT-3) produced personalized, natural-sounding dialogues, enabling the robot to respond to user queries, provide emotional support, or even suggest social activities tailored to the user's emotional and cognitive state.

4. **Learning and Adaptation**: The robot continuously learned from each interaction, adjusting its behavior based on feedback such as the user's preferences, response to certain activities, or emotional state over time.

Results

The implementation of **Generative AI** in the human-robot interaction system led to several positive outcomes:

1. **Improved Emotional Awareness**: The robot was able to accurately detect and respond to changes in the user's emotional state, offering more empathetic and appropriate responses. For instance, when users seemed lonely or upset, the robot could engage in comforting dialogue or suggest activities to lift their mood.

2. **Enhanced Communication**: The robot's ability to generate natural, contextually appropriate responses greatly improved the quality of interactions. Users

felt like they were engaging in a conversation rather than issuing commands, which made the experience feel more human-like and comfortable.

3. **Increased Adaptability**: The robot showed increased adaptability in meeting individual users' needs. Over time, it learned each person's preferences and developed a personalized interaction style that better suited their emotional and social needs.

4. **User Satisfaction**: The elderly individuals who interacted with the robot reported higher satisfaction levels compared to traditional robotic assistants, particularly in terms of feeling "heard" and "understood." Many users also found the robot's companionship to be a significant improvement in their daily lives, helping reduce feelings of isolation.

Challenges and Limitations

Despite the positive results, there were challenges:

- **Cultural and Social Sensitivity**: The robot's emotional recognition model may not have fully captured cultural or individual differences in how emotions are expressed, which could have led to misunderstandings in certain contexts.

- **Computational Load**: Real-time emotion recognition and response generation required significant computational resources, which posed challenges in making the system lightweight and efficient for continuous deployment.

- **Long-Term Adaptation**: While the robot was able to learn from interactions, the rate at which it could adapt to new users or drastically changing circumstances (e.g., sudden shifts in emotional state) could still be slow.

Future Directions

Future improvements could focus on:

- **Better Emotion Recognition**: Incorporating multimodal sensors (e.g., wearables) to capture a wider range of emotional cues.

- **Expanded NLP Capabilities**: Enhancing the robot's ability to handle more complex, open-ended conversations, including understanding sarcasm or indirect speech.

- **Scalability**: Improving the system to allow for deployment in a wide range of settings beyond elderly care, such as customer service or education, where HRI plays a critical role.

Conclusion

Generative AI has the potential to revolutionize **Human-Robot Interaction**, enabling robots to engage more meaningfully with humans by recognizing emotions, generating contextually appropriate responses, and adapting over time. The use of advanced models like **VAEs** and **transformers** allows for more flexible, empathetic, and intelligent interactions, leading to increased satisfaction and effectiveness in applications such as elderly care, healthcare, and customer service. As AI continues to evolve, these systems will become even more capable of seamlessly integrating into human environments and providing valuable assistance in a wide variety of contexts.

This case study demonstrates the significant impact **Generative AI** can have on enhancing human-robot interactions, making robots more intelligent, empathetic, and adaptive to human needs.

10.4 Case Study: Generative AI, Robotics, and Autonomous Systems

Introduction

Generative AI is revolutionizing robotics and autonomous systems by enabling robots to generate realistic simulations, autonomously plan tasks, and improve interaction with the environment. The combination of **Generative AI** and **Robotics** facilitates the development of robots that not only execute predefined tasks but also adapt and optimize their behavior based on complex, dynamic environments. One key area where this integration has been transformative is in **autonomous systems**—machines that can operate independently, without human intervention, and complete tasks in the physical world. This case study will explore how **Generative AI** has been utilized to enhance autonomous systems in a **warehouse automation** scenario.

Background

In modern logistics, warehouses are key nodes in supply chains, and their efficiency is critical for managing inventory, shipping, and handling. Traditional automation systems rely on **pre-programmed robots** to perform specific tasks like picking, sorting, and transporting goods. However, as warehouse environments grow more complex and dynamic, there is a need for more adaptive, flexible robots that can handle unexpected changes, such as new product types, shifting stock locations, or environmental disruptions.

A leading logistics company sought to enhance their warehouse automation by deploying **generative AI-based**

autonomous robots to improve efficiency and adapt to changing circumstances without human intervention.

Problem

Traditional warehouse robots faced several limitations:

- **Static behavior**: Robots were pre-programmed to follow specific tasks and paths. This rigid behavior prevented them from handling unexpected events like sudden layout changes, unanticipated inventory changes, or obstacles in the environment.

- **Limited flexibility**: Robots could not adapt to varying environments or learn from new experiences. For example, if a robot faced an obstacle, it would often stop and require manual intervention to resume its task.

- **Inefficiency in complex tasks**: Handling complex, multi-step operations (such as locating and retrieving items from dynamically changing locations) required intensive programming and did not scale well as the warehouse grew.

These limitations hindered the scalability and adaptability of warehouse automation systems.

Generative AI Solution

To solve these challenges, the company implemented **Generative AI** within its autonomous robots, enabling them to dynamically adjust to new tasks and environments. The system incorporated several **Generative AI algorithms**, including **Generative Adversarial Networks (GANs)** and

Variational Autoencoders (VAEs), to enable the robots to learn and simulate realistic scenarios.

Here's how generative AI was applied:

1. **Generative Simulation for Path Planning**:
   - **Generative AI** was used to create simulated environments where robots could learn and test their navigation strategies before deploying them in real-world scenarios. For example, a **Generative Adversarial Network (GAN)** was trained on vast amounts of warehouse layout data to generate new possible obstacles, inventory configurations, and paths.

   - These simulations helped the robots adapt to changes such as temporary blockages, changing inventory, or different robot positions. By experiencing various simulated scenarios, robots learned to develop strategies to navigate efficiently in an ever-changing environment.

2. **Autonomous Task Generation and Execution**:
   - **Generative AI** was used to dynamically generate tasks for the robots based on real-time data. For example, when the system detected a high-priority shipment, the robots could autonomously create a sequence of actions to locate, pick, and transport the necessary items, optimizing task execution in the context of available resources.

- o By utilizing **reinforcement learning** (RL) combined with generative models, robots continuously refined their task generation process to maximize efficiency, taking into account factors like time, energy consumption, and task complexity.

3. **Real-Time Adaptation and Self-Improvement**:

   - o The robots used **Variational Autoencoders (VAEs)** to process sensory data (e.g., from cameras, LIDAR, or other sensors) to detect and adapt to changes in their environment. The **VAE** architecture was applied to detect unexpected objects or changes in layout and simulate potential outcomes, helping the robots plan new paths or task sequences based on new observations.

   - o For instance, when an unexpected pile of boxes obstructed the robot's path, the robot used **generative models** to simulate alternative routes, taking into account the most efficient solution. This allowed the robot to reroute in real-time without needing human input.

4. **Behavioral Flexibility**:

   - o Using generative models, robots were able to exhibit **flexible behaviors** based on environmental conditions. If a robot detected a human worker nearby, it could generate responses such as slowing down, adjusting its path, or politely signaling its intention. This level of interaction created a more **cooperative and safe work environment** in the warehouse.

○ Additionally, the robots used generative algorithms to predict and **model human behavior**. By anticipating the actions of nearby humans, the robots adjusted their own behavior in real-time, optimizing both their tasks and interactions with human operators.

Implementation

The system was deployed in the warehouse, where several autonomous robots, equipped with generative AI-based navigation, task allocation, and decision-making models, began their operations. The workflow was as follows:

1. **Real-Time Data Gathering**: Robots gathered data from sensors, cameras, and LIDAR systems to build a real-time map of the warehouse environment. This map was continually updated to reflect any new obstacles, layout changes, or inventory shifts.

2. **Simulation-Based Task Generation**: Based on the current state of the warehouse and the robots' objectives, **generative models** were used to generate task sequences. These tasks included locating items, navigating aisles, avoiding obstacles, and delivering goods to specific locations.

3. **Continuous Learning and Adaptation**: As the robots completed tasks, they fed data back into a central learning system. The system used this data to

fine-tune the robots' models, allowing them to adapt and improve based on the success or failure of previous actions. For example, if a robot frequently encountered obstacles in a particular area, the system would adjust the robot's path-planning strategy for future operations.

4. **Scalable and Flexible Deployment**: The system could easily scale as new robots were added to the fleet. The **generative AI models** ensured that even newly deployed robots could quickly integrate into the workflow without requiring significant retraining or reprogramming.

Results

The deployment of **Generative AI in autonomous robots** yielded impressive results:

1. **Improved Efficiency**: Robots were able to complete tasks faster and with more efficiency due to their ability to dynamically adapt to changing environments. By continuously optimizing their paths and task execution strategies, they reduced the time taken for each operation.

2. **Higher Flexibility and Scalability**: The robots' ability to learn from experience and adjust to new situations allowed the system to scale with ease. When the warehouse expanded or underwent layout changes, the robots could quickly adjust to the new environment, reducing downtime.

3. **Real-Time Adaptation**: The robots demonstrated significant improvements in **real-time decision-**

making. For instance, when a robot encountered a temporary obstruction, it was able to generate and execute alternative paths autonomously, without human intervention.

4. **Cost Savings**: By automating more tasks and improving efficiency, the company reduced labor costs. Additionally, the AI-powered robots minimized operational errors and downtime, leading to substantial cost savings.

5. **Better Human-Robot Collaboration**: The robots' ability to adapt to human workers' behavior and adjust their interactions accordingly improved safety and cooperation in the warehouse. Human workers felt more comfortable and safer, knowing the robots could predict their movements and adjust behavior accordingly.

Challenges and Limitations

While the system delivered impressive results, there were some challenges:

1. **Complexity in Model Training**: The training of generative models for real-world environments required substantial computational resources and time. Ensuring the models generalized well across different scenarios was a key challenge.

2. **Environmental Variability**: While the system adapted well to common changes in the warehouse environment, rare or extreme disruptions still presented difficulties. For example, if the layout was radically altered or an entirely new type of item was

introduced, the robots sometimes struggled to optimize their task allocation.

3. **Communication Overhead**: As the number of robots increased, communication among them became more complex, requiring sophisticated protocols to prevent network congestion and delays.

Future Directions

To enhance the performance of these systems, future improvements could focus on:

- **Multi-Robot Coordination**: Further developing generative models for more effective coordination and collaboration between robots to handle more complex tasks that involve multiple agents.

- **Improved Simulation Training**: Enhancing the generative simulation capabilities to better model extreme or rare scenarios, ensuring that robots are prepared for a wider range of events.

- **Energy Efficiency**: Incorporating AI-based strategies to optimize energy consumption during operation, which could help further reduce costs.

Conclusion

Generative AI has the potential to dramatically enhance the performance of autonomous systems by enabling them to generate realistic simulations, adapt to real-time changes, and improve decision-making. In the case of warehouse automation, the integration of **generative AI** with robotics has led to greater efficiency, scalability, and adaptability, making it possible for robots to handle dynamic and complex environments autonomously. As these technologies continue to evolve, we can expect further improvements in the capabilities of autonomous systems across industries, leading to smarter, more adaptable robots that can work seamlessly in a wide range of real-world applications.

10.5 Case Study: Generative Adversarial Networks (GANs) in Robotics

Introduction

Generative Adversarial Networks (GANs) have become a transformative force in the field of artificial intelligence, and their application in **robotics** has opened up new possibilities for enhancing robot capabilities, particularly in environments where data is scarce or dynamic. In robotics, **GANs** can be used for tasks ranging from improving simulation data for training, creating new robot behaviors, enhancing vision systems, and improving the decision-making processes of autonomous robots.

This case study focuses on how GANs have been applied to **robotic perception** and **simulation-based training** for autonomous robots, particularly in **industrial settings** such as automated warehouses. The goal of using GANs in this context is to generate realistic synthetic data that can be used to train robots in environments that are too dangerous, rare, or costly to simulate in real life.

Background

Autonomous robots often rely on large datasets to train their vision systems and control algorithms. However, acquiring sufficient real-world data for training can be expensive and time-consuming. Moreover, some real-world scenarios are difficult to recreate during training, such as rare or hazardous situations.

The **robot perception system**—particularly **computer vision**—is critical for robots to navigate, interact with objects, and perform tasks such as picking, sorting, or avoiding obstacles. In environments like warehouses, these robots must process visual input and adapt in real-time to new or unexpected situations. Using GANs to generate synthetic training data can help overcome the limitations of limited real-world data.

Problem

Traditional robot training methods often face several issues:

1. **Insufficient Training Data**: Gathering real-world data to train robots in dynamic environments can be time-consuming and costly. Moreover, certain edge cases or rare events (e.g., unexpected objects or rare failures) may not be well-represented in real-world datasets.

2. **Hazardous Environments**: Some environments are dangerous for robots to operate in while being trained, such as hazardous waste areas, high-risk manufacturing plants, or locations with dynamic obstacles. In such cases, physical testing can be dangerous or prohibitively expensive.

3. **Data Scarcity for Edge Cases**: Robots may fail to recognize unusual objects or encounter unexpected conditions (e.g., lighting changes or unusual object shapes). In such cases, it is difficult to manually generate a dataset to train these models.

To address these issues, the company chose to implement **Generative Adversarial Networks (GANs)** as a solution for creating synthetic data to train the robots' vision systems and improve the robots' ability to adapt to unpredictable environments.

Generative Adversarial Networks (GANs) Solution

Generative Adversarial Networks (GANs) consist of two neural networks: a **generator** and a **discriminator**. The generator creates synthetic data (e.g., images), while the discriminator evaluates how real the generated data is compared to actual data. Through this adversarial process, the generator learns to create increasingly realistic data that can be used to train other machine learning models.

In this case, GANs were applied in the following ways:

1. **Synthetic Image Generation for Perception**:

    o   GANs were used to generate realistic images that simulated a wide variety of environments and scenarios, such as different lighting conditions, weather effects (rain, fog), and object occlusions. These synthetic images served as a diverse dataset to train the robot's perception system, allowing it to recognize and interact with objects even in challenging conditions.

    o   The GANs were trained on real-world images captured by the robots' cameras and vision sensors. The generated images mimicked these real-world conditions, but with the added benefit of being able to generate vast quantities of data, including rare and difficult-to-represent scenarios, such as an item being partially obstructed by other objects or different textures on a surface.

2. **Simulating Rare Events and Edge Cases**:

- Rare or high-risk situations, like sudden environmental changes (e.g., an object falling in front of the robot) or unusual lighting (e.g., a flash of light from a nearby window), were often underrepresented in the real-world data. GANs were used to generate synthetic images of these edge cases, allowing robots to learn how to handle such rare events.

- This enabled the robot to train in simulations of extreme or hazardous conditions that would be too dangerous or impractical to create in a physical setting.

3. **Improved Visual Inspection for Object Recognition**:

- In robotic tasks such as **picking and sorting**, robots must identify and classify objects accurately. By using GANs, the robots were exposed to various object configurations, even if those configurations were not present in the training set. This enhanced the robot's ability to recognize objects in a wider range of positions, orientations, and environmental contexts.

- The generated data not only helped train the robots to recognize typical objects but also unfamiliar ones, expanding their ability to deal with a broader variety of objects.

4. **Enhancing Path Planning and Decision-Making**:

- o Beyond image generation, GANs were used to simulate **robot movements** within a physical space. The generator created simulated paths and trajectories based on real-world conditions, such as warehouse layouts, obstacles, and robot movement patterns. This allowed the robots to train their **path planning algorithms** in synthetic yet realistic scenarios before deploying them in real-world environments.

- o By simulating scenarios where robots faced dynamic obstacles or shifting paths (e.g., a robot suddenly having to avoid a person or another robot), the GANs helped improve the robots' decision-making capabilities.

Implementation Process

1. **Data Collection and Preprocessing**:

   - o The first step involved collecting real-world data using the robot's onboard cameras and sensors in the warehouse. These images were preprocessed (e.g., by adjusting lighting conditions, orientations, and object occlusion) to create diverse data inputs for the GANs to learn from.

2. **Training the GAN Model**:

   - o The GAN was trained on a large dataset of real-world images, which included varied lighting, object shapes, and environmental conditions. The goal was for the generator to produce synthetic images that mimicked these real-world conditions with high fidelity.

- o Training involved a back-and-forth process: the generator produced synthetic images, and the discriminator evaluated how similar they were to the real-world images. Over time, the generator improved its output, producing data that was close enough to real images to be useful for training other machine learning algorithms, such as object detection and path planning.

3. **Deployment in Robotics**:

- o Once the GANs were sufficiently trained, the synthetic images generated by the GAN were fed into the robot's vision system. These images were used to train the robots to recognize objects and navigate the warehouse environment.

- o The robots were able to simulate interactions with a variety of objects under different conditions and adapt their behavior to handle edge cases and rare events. This improved their efficiency in real-world tasks such as sorting, item picking, and delivery.

4. **Continuous Improvement**:

- o The system included a feedback loop where robots continued to learn from real-world operations. When the robots encountered new situations that were not well-represented in the synthetic data, the GANs were updated with new real-world data to improve future simulations and ensure the robots could continue to adapt to changing environments.

Results

The use of GANs in the robotic perception system led to several positive outcomes:

1. **Improved Object Recognition**: Robots were able to recognize objects with higher accuracy, even in challenging lighting conditions or when objects were partially occluded. This enhanced the robots' ability to operate in dynamic and unpredictable environments.

2. **Increased Efficiency**: By utilizing synthetic data to train the robots, the time required for data collection was dramatically reduced. Robots could be trained faster and more effectively without the need for large amounts of real-world data.

3. **Adaptation to Edge Cases**: The robots were able to handle rare or unexpected situations, such as interacting with newly introduced items or navigating around temporary obstacles. This capability greatly improved the robots' reliability and robustness in real-world operations.

4. **Cost Savings**: The use of synthetic data reduced the need for physical testing in potentially dangerous or hard-to-reach environments, leading to significant cost savings. Moreover, by training the robots more

effectively, the overall operational efficiency improved, reducing downtime and errors.

Challenges and Limitations

1. **Model Complexity**: GANs are computationally intensive and require significant processing power to generate high-quality synthetic data. Fine-tuning the GAN model to generate realistic images and simulate real-world conditions took considerable time and resources.

2. **Generalization to New Environments**: While GANs helped generate data for many scenarios, the challenge of ensuring that synthetic data generalizes well to completely new environments (e.g., entirely different warehouse layouts) still exists. The robots required ongoing refinement to adapt to completely unfamiliar scenarios.

3. **Data Distribution Issues**: GANs rely on a diverse dataset, and if the real-world data used for training was not diverse enough, the generated synthetic data might not adequately cover all possible scenarios, leading to gaps in the robot's learning.

Future Directions

- **Improved GAN Architectures**: New advancements in GAN architectures, such as **StyleGANs** or **CycleGANs**, may improve the realism and diversity of synthetic data, allowing robots to adapt to even more complex environments.

- **Hybrid Models**: Combining GANs with other techniques, such as reinforcement learning (RL) and

transfer learning, could further enhance robot adaptation by allowing them to continually refine their decision-making processes based on real-time feedback.

- **Real-Time Data Augmentation**: Future systems may incorporate real-time GAN-based data augmentation, where robots generate synthetic data on-the-fly during operation, improving adaptability without requiring extensive retraining.

Conclusion

The application of **Generative Adversarial Networks (GANs)** in robotics has shown significant potential in enhancing the capabilities of autonomous systems. By enabling robots to generate and utilize synthetic data for training, particularly in the areas of object recognition, navigation, and decision-making, GANs help improve efficiency, safety, and adaptability. As the technology continues to evolve, GANs are likely to play an even more pivotal role in creating intelligent, autonomous robots capable of handling increasingly complex real-world tasks.

10.6 Case Study: Variational Autoencoders (VAEs) and Their Application in Robotics

Introduction

In the rapidly advancing field of robotics, one of the most critical challenges is enabling robots to understand and adapt to the complex, dynamic environments in which they operate. Robots must efficiently process sensory data, navigate their surroundings, and make decisions in real time. **Variational Autoencoders (VAEs)**, a deep learning model, have emerged as an effective tool for addressing many of these challenges, particularly in terms of perception, learning, and adaptation in robotics.

A **Variational Autoencoder (VAE)** is a generative model that learns to represent complex data distributions in a compressed form. It excels at tasks such as anomaly detection, data denoising, and generating new data points. In robotics, VAEs can be used for a variety of purposes, including generating high-quality representations of sensor data, learning robotic control policies, and improving robot learning from limited or noisy data.

This case study explores how **VAEs** have been applied in **robot perception** and **robot learning** in an industrial setting, specifically in a warehouse automation scenario. By utilizing VAEs, the robots were able to improve their ability to process sensor data and adapt to new tasks without requiring large amounts of labeled training data.

Background

In an industrial warehouse setting, robots are often tasked with performing complex tasks such as **object recognition**,

path planning, and **pick-and-place operations**. These tasks require the robots to process and understand data from a variety of sensors, such as **cameras**, **LIDAR**, and **ultrasonic sensors**. However, the data from these sensors can be noisy, incomplete, or difficult to interpret, making it challenging for robots to function optimally in real-world environments.

Furthermore, warehouses are often dynamic environments with changing layouts, moving obstacles (e.g., people or other robots), and unpredictable conditions. Therefore, robots must be able to learn quickly from limited or noisy data and adapt to new situations.

In this case study, a warehouse automation company integrated **Variational Autoencoders (VAEs)** into their robots' systems to enhance their ability to interpret sensor data, learn new tasks efficiently, and adapt to changing conditions in the warehouse.

Problem

1. **Noisy and Incomplete Data**: Robots in the warehouse relied on sensor data to navigate and recognize objects. However, the sensor data was often noisy, incomplete, or corrupted due to environmental factors such as dust, lighting conditions, or occlusions. This made it difficult for the robots to accurately interpret the world around them.

2. **Limited Training Data**: Collecting large amounts of labeled training data for the robots' machine learning models was costly and time-consuming. In many

cases, the robots needed to adapt to new tasks or environments with limited or sparse data.

3. **Generalization to Unseen Environments**: The robots had difficulty generalizing to new or unseen environments, such as a rearranged warehouse layout or the introduction of new types of objects. This limited their flexibility and required frequent retraining.

Solution: Application of Variational Autoencoders (VAEs)

Variational Autoencoders (VAEs) were implemented to address these challenges in several key areas of robot operation:

1. **Data Representation and Noise Reduction**:

   o The VAE was used to learn a **low-dimensional latent representation** of the sensor data, allowing the robot to compress complex, high-dimensional data (e.g., images or point clouds) into a more compact and interpretable form. This representation captured the essential features of the data while discarding noise and irrelevant information.

   o For example, VAE models were applied to image data captured by the robot's cameras. The VAE learned to map the high-dimensional image data into a lower-dimensional space, where the most critical features (such as object shapes, sizes, and orientations) were preserved. This helped the robot make better decisions in environments with poor visibility or lighting conditions.

2. **Anomaly Detection and Fault Tolerance**:
   o VAEs were trained to identify **anomalous sensor readings** that might indicate problems with the robot's sensors, its environment, or its tasks. By learning the normal data distribution, the VAE could detect when sensor data deviated from the expected pattern (e.g., due to sensor malfunctions or unexpected environmental changes).

   o For example, if the robot's cameras captured unusual images (such as an obstruction in the path or a new type of object), the VAE could flag these as anomalies. The robot could then adapt its behavior by rerouting or adjusting its task sequence, ensuring that it continued to operate safely and efficiently.

3. **Learning from Sparse Data**:
   o In situations where large amounts of labeled training data were not available, VAEs were used to generate **synthetic data**. By learning the underlying distribution of data from a small amount of labeled examples, the VAE could generate additional examples that were similar to the real data. This synthetic data could then be used to train other models, such

as object detection networks, reducing the need for extensive data collection.

- o For instance, when the robots encountered new objects that had not been seen before, the VAE could generate realistic variations of those objects, including changes in appearance, lighting, or occlusions. This helped the robot's vision system generalize to new objects without requiring extensive retraining.

4. **Task Adaptation and Generalization**:

- o VAEs were employed to help the robots **generalize** to new tasks or environments by learning a **shared latent space** that could accommodate various robot configurations, tasks, and environments. For example, if the robot was trained in a specific warehouse layout, the VAE could generate latent representations of new environments, allowing the robot to adapt its control policies to the new space.

- o The VAE's ability to capture underlying patterns allowed robots to **transfer knowledge** from one environment to another without needing extensive retraining. This improved their flexibility and efficiency when adapting to new layouts or tasks.

Implementation Process

1. **Data Collection and Preprocessing**:

o The robots were equipped with cameras, LIDAR, and other sensors to collect data from the warehouse environment. This raw data was preprocessed to remove noise and align it with the robot's task (e.g., object detection, path planning).

2. **Training the VAE Model**:

o A **VAE model** was trained on the collected sensor data (e.g., images, depth maps, etc.). The training process involved learning the **latent space** of the data, which could capture the essential features and patterns in the input data while reducing dimensionality.

o The VAE was trained to map sensor data (such as camera images) to a lower-dimensional latent space, where it could more easily recognize objects and navigate in the warehouse.

3. **Integration with Robot Control System**:

o Once the VAE model was trained, it was integrated into the robot's control system. The robot's perception system used the VAE to process sensor data, detect anomalies, and adapt to new environments or tasks based on the latent representations generated by the VAE.

o For example, when a robot encountered a new object, the VAE would generate a latent representation of the object, and the robot's task planner would use this representation to plan the appropriate action (e.g., pick, avoid, or move the object).

4. **Continuous Learning**:

   o The VAE was part of a **continuous learning loop**, where the robots updated their models based on real-world experiences. This allowed them to improve over time and adapt to changing environments without requiring a complete retraining process.

Results

The implementation of **Variational Autoencoders (VAEs)** in the warehouse robots resulted in several key improvements:

1. **Enhanced Perception**: The VAE-enabled robots were able to process noisy and incomplete sensor data more effectively. They learned to focus on the most relevant features of the environment, improving their object recognition capabilities even in challenging conditions.

2. **Improved Adaptation to New Tasks**: The robots showed increased ability to adapt to new environments and tasks. By leveraging the shared latent space learned by the VAE, the robots were able to generalize to new layouts, environments, and objects with minimal retraining.

3. **Data Efficiency**: The VAE allowed the robots to learn from limited data, reducing the need for extensive labeled datasets. The ability to generate

synthetic data meant the robots could continue to improve even when only a small amount of real-world data was available.

4. **Fault Detection and Safety**: The anomaly detection capabilities of the VAE helped identify potential issues with the robot's sensors or environment, improving fault tolerance and safety. For example, if the robot encountered an unexpected obstacle, the VAE could flag it as an anomaly, prompting the robot to take corrective action.

Challenges and Limitations

While the VAE-based solution delivered significant benefits, there were also challenges:

1. **Training Complexity**: Training the VAE models on large amounts of high-dimensional sensor data was computationally intensive and required specialized hardware for efficient processing.

2. **Generalization to Highly Unstructured Environments**: While VAEs were effective in many scenarios, there were challenges in environments with highly dynamic or unstructured conditions, where the variability of objects or obstacles was difficult to model.

3. **Real-Time Processing**: While VAEs can process data efficiently, real-time processing requirements in fast-paced environments (such as picking and placing in a busy warehouse) meant that optimizing the model's inference speed was critical.

Future Directions

- **Hybrid Models**: Combining VAEs with other machine learning models, such as reinforcement learning or deep neural networks, could further improve robot adaptation and learning capabilities.

- **Online Learning**: Developing VAE models that can continuously update and adapt in real-time based on new sensor data would improve robots' ability to learn and adapt to continuously changing environments.

- **Multi-Robot Systems**: VAEs could be extended to multi-robot systems, where robots learn from each other's experiences and share knowledge, improving coordination and efficiency.

Conclusion

The application of **Variational Autoencoders (VAEs)** in robotics has proven to be a valuable tool for improving **perception**, **task adaptation**, and **learning efficiency** in complex, dynamic environments. By enabling robots to process noisy sensor data, detect anomalies, and adapt to new tasks with limited data, VAEs have enhanced the robots' ability to operate autonomously and efficiently in industrial settings like warehouses. As the technology continues to evolve, VAEs are likely to play an even more significant role in advancing robot learning and adaptability.